Favorite Seafood Recipes

by
Sally Murphy Morris

REVISED EDITION

A Nitty Gritty® Cookbook

Printed in the United States of America.

ISBN 1-55867-000-9

Designed by Mike Nelson
Edited by Jackie Walsh
Photographs by Glen Millward
Food Stylist: Bobbie Greenlaw

TABLE OF CONTENTS

SERVE CREATIVE, EASY, NUTRITIOUS MEALS — COLLECT THEM ALL

The Bread Machine Cookbook
The Kid's Microwave Cookbook
15-Minute Meals for 1 or 2
Recipes for the 9x13 Pan
Turkey, The Magic Ingredient
Chocolate Cherry Tortes and Other Lowfat
   Delights
Lowfat American Favorites
Lowfat International Cuisine
The Hunk Cookbook
Now That's Italian!
Fabulous Fiber Cookery
Low Salt, Low Sugar, Low Fat Desserts
What's for Breakfast?
Healthy Cooking on the Run
Healthy Snacks for Kids
Creative Soups & Salads
Quick & Easy Pasta Recipes
Muffins, Nut Breads and More
The Barbecue Book
The Wok
New Ways with Your Wok

Quiche & Soufflé Cookbook
Easy Microwave Cooking
Compleat American Housewife 1787
Cooking for 1 or 2
Brunch
Cocktails & Hors d'Oeuvres
Meals in Minutes
New Ways to Enjoy Chicken
Favorite Seafood Recipes
No Salt, No Sugar, No Fat Cookbook
The Fresh Vegetable Cookbook
Modern Ice Cream Recipes
Crepes & Omelets
Time-Saving Gourmet Cooking
New International Fondue Cookbook
Extra-Special Crockery Pot Recipes
Favorite Cookie Recipes
Authentic Mexican Cooking
Fisherman's Wharf Cookbook
The Kid's Cookbook
The Best of Nitty Gritty
The Creative Lunch Box

Write or call for our free catalog.
Bristol Publishing Enterprises, Inc.
P.O. Box 1737, San Leandro, CA 94577
(800)346-4889   or (415)895-4461

INTRODUCTION

Shopping for seafood is a real adventure. Of more than 25,000 named varieties, 350 or more are available at various times to sportsfishermen and the retail trade. This means you will have an enormous variety from which to choose.

You will be faced with many decisions. Will you buy fresh, frozen or canned fish? Will you choose fin fish or shell fish? Will you cook it in the oven, the microwave, on the grill or in a wok? Do you select fish for all the popularly touted health reasons, because you love the taste, or because you want variety in your diet? Perhaps you are choosing fish because it is a high quality, lowfat protein at a reasonable price. Or you may choose it because most methods require a brief cooking time which makes it perfect for today's busy families.

Whatever the reason, there are two recommendations to follow. First, make friends with your fishmonger. He is usually a walking encyclopedia of information and will be flattered if you ask his advice. Take it, but remember the second recommendation, and the most important in fish cookery: **do not overcook!**

Most commonly available varieties of fish are covered in this book. You may substitute any fish within the fish family (see **Fish Families**, page 21, or the Index), or within the list of fish with similar fat content (see **Fat Content of Fish**, page 2). Once you are experienced you may even switch lean fish for fat, but lean fish may require more basting.

FAT CONTENT OF FISH

Lean Fish (up to 5% fat)

bass (all)
brook trout
cod
dolphin (mahimahi)
flounder (or flatfish)
haddock
halibut
mullet
perch (all)
pompano
shark
snapper (including opakapaka)
sole (or flatfish)
swordfish
tilefish
whitefish

Fat or Oily Fish (more than 5% fat)

carp
catfish
cod (including hake, pollock)
drum (including sheepshead)
herring
mackerel (including tuna)
pike (including muskie)
porgy
red snapper
salmon
smelt
striped bass
sturgeon
trout

THE "HOW TO'S" OF SELECTING AND PREPARING FISH

How to Judge Freshness

Before you buy fish, check it closely. Don't buy it if it can't pass these tests:

Eyes   Clear, bright and bulging. Old fish have sunken, cloudy eyes.
Gills   Red, free of slime and odor. Old fish are gray, then brown, then green.
Scales   Tightly adhered to skin with a marked sheen.
Flesh   Firm, elastic, springs back when touched. Old skin is dry and browned.
Odor   Fresh, not objectionable.

How Much Fish to Buy

Because appetites vary greatly, this is strictly a guide.

Whole	1 lb. per serving
Dressed	1/2 lb. per serving
Steaks, fillets, sticks	1/3 lb. per serving

Fish Forms Prior to Cooking

Become familiar with these common fish forms, whether you are shopping, cooking or even going out to dinner.

Whole
This is the least expensive form of fish, although only 45% of it is edible. This is the fish just as it comes from the water.

Drawn or Cleaned:
This is the whole fish with entrails (innards) removed. It is about 48% edible.

Dressed:
This is the whole fish with entrails, scales and fins removed. Sometimes the tail and/or head have been removed. It is about 67% edible.

Steaks and Chunks:
These are cross sections of fish with only a small piece of bone in each section. Fish steaks are usually 1 inch thick. Fish chunks are usually 4 to 6 inches in diameter. These forms are about 84% edible.

Fillets:
These are meaty slices of fish, cut lengthwise from just behind the head to the tail. They are nearly boneless and may be skinless. They are almost 100% edible.

Butterfly:
This is a double fillet, with the two sides connected at the backbone. It is nearly boneless. Because fish is not usually marketed in this form, you'll probably have to specially order it from your fishmonger. A butterfly fillet is almost 100% edible.

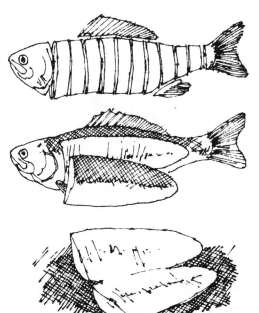

Fingers:
These are 1/2-inch wide strips, cut vertically, against the grain of fish fillets. They are usually sold frozen in a breading. They are 100% edible.

Sticks or Portions:
These are large (about 3 inches by 7 inches), rectangular strips of fish, cut from commercially frozen blocks of fillets. They too are usually sold frozen in a breading. They are 100% edible.

How to Store Fish

Fish deteriorates rapidly. The process begins as soon as it leaves the water, so handling fish with care is important. If you are catching your own, put it on ice immediately. If you purchase it at the market, return home as quickly as possible. When you arrive home, treat the fish in one of the following ways:

1. If you are not planning on eating the fish within 2 days, freeze it. The proper procedure for this is first to dress the fish (see page 8). Second, wrap the fish in plastic bags. Third, wrap the fish again using freezer paper. Date and label your fish. Store it no more than 1 month. Avoid freezing fish whenever possible. Freezing robs the fish of its delicate taste and texture, oftentimes.

2. If you plan on eating your fish within 2 days, dress it (see page 8), wrap it well, and store it in the coolest part of your refrigerator.

How to Prepare Fish for Cooking

If you don't plan on catching your own, you'll probably never have to clean a fish. Your fishmonger will do it for you. But, if you like to fish or have a friend who sometimes gives you fresh fish, you'll need to know the proper procedure.

You should have: A 6-inch fillet knife, a large cutting board, a fish scaler or spoon and some old newspapers.

Scaling:

Because fish scales have a tendency to "fly" all over the kitchen, some people prefer to scale their fish outside. Whether you do it outside or inside, follow these steps. First, soak the fish in salt water for five minutes. This makes scaling easier. Then place wet fish on cutting board. Keep newspaper spread out, so that you can put the scales in it as they collect. Hold the fish tail with one hand. Pick up the scaler or spoon with your other hand. Then, beginning at the tail, carefully scrape toward the head to remove the scales. Make sure all scales are removed.

Dressing:

Also known as cleaning, gutting or drawing. To remove the entrails, make a belly cut from the anal or ventral fin to the pelvic fin (see page 13).

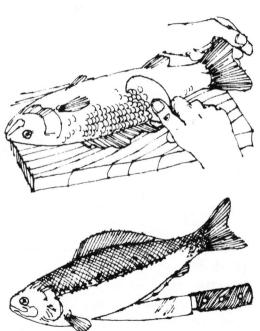

On a large fish, make a second cut from gill to gill, across the throat.

Using the point of your knife, pull out and discard the internal organs.

Unless your fish is very small and you plan to pan fry it, cut off the tail.

Remove the head, but don't throw it away! Save it for fish stock (see page 134).

Remove pectoral fins by cutting behind the gills and collarbone.

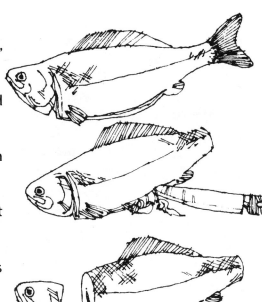

Continued

Dressing Continued

Remove the backbone by cutting on each side of the dorsal fin.

Pull the fin toward head. It should come out. If your fish is large, you may have to use a coping saw or cleaver to sever the backbone before it can be removed.

Remove the remaining fins by making an incision (a cut) around each. Pull them free. Rinse to remove any blood.

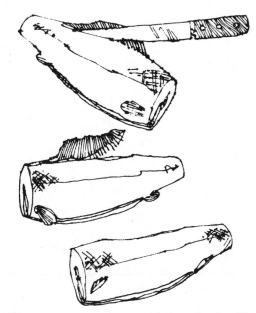

Your fish is now dressed. You may continue to operate on it, or cook it whole. If you wish to fillet, skin or cut your fish into steaks, follow these steps.

Filleting:

You may fillet fish without cleaning it. But, if the skin is to be left on, it must be scaled and gilled. To fillet, place fish on cutting board with belly side of fish closest to your body. With a fillet knife, make an incision just behind the pectoral fin. Slide the knife along the rib cage, from head to tail, using a sawing motion. The fillet should come off in one piece. Turn the fish over and repeat.

Skinning:

To skin the fish, work the knife between the flesh and the skin at the tail. While holding the tail in one hand, pull the skin against the knife and draw knife away from tail. Save all scraps for stock (see page 134).

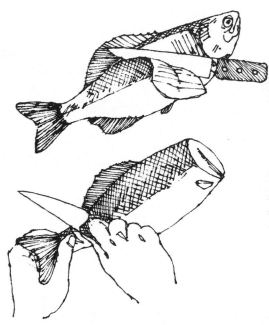

Filleting Flatfish:

Due to their large size and nearly flat shape, special instructions are needed to fillet flatfish. They require two horizontal cuts. Cut down to backbone, behind the head (cut 1). With the knife almost horizontal, slide it along the rib cage from the nape to the tail (cut 2). Repeat on other side. This should release the bones.

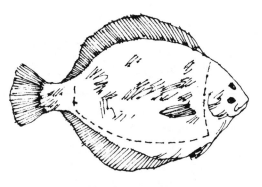

Cutting Steaks:

Cut 1-inch cross sections of dressed fish by slicing down through backbone with a heavy knife or cleaver. If the backbone is thick, either tap the knife with a mallet, or use a coping saw.

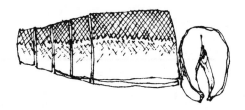

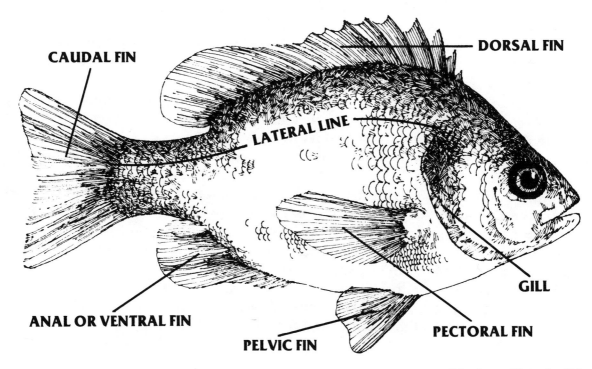

CAUDAL FIN

DORSAL FIN

LATERAL LINE

ANAL OR VENTRAL FIN

PELVIC FIN

PECTORAL FIN

GILL

BASIC WAYS OF COOKING FISH

DON'T OVERCOOK! This is the most important advice to be given about the cooking of fish. Excess cooking will only dry it out and make it flavorless. Fish is naturally tender. It should be cooked just to firm the flesh.

All fish, either fillets, steaks or whole fish, should be cooked according to the Consumer Division of the Canadian Fisheries and Marine Service Rule, better known as the **Canadian Rule: Measure the fish at its thickest point—its depth, not across the fish—and cook it exactly 10 minutes per inch. If fish is 1/2-inch thick, cook 5 minutes; if it is 1-inch thick, cook 10 minutes; if it is 1-1/2-inches thick, cook 15 minutes; etc. This is foolproof and eliminates all that testing and flaking and the fish looks prettier as a result. The Canadian Rule applies to every sort of preparation—baking, broiling, braising, sauteing, frying, poaching and steaming.** If the fish you are using is still frozen, double the time—20 minutes per inch of thickness, plus or minus any fraction thereof. **The Canadian Rule does not apply to shellfish.**

For best results know the properties of your fish before you cook it. Is it lean or fat; mild or strong flavored? The Fish Families Chart beginning on page 22 will help you choose the cooking method best suited for the type of fish you are using.

BAKING

Cleaned, dressed whole fish, steaks and fillets bake well. The flavor of a baked, whole fish is improved when the head and tail are left on. If you plan to stuff the fish, fill it only 2/3 full to allow for expansion. For easy clean-up, line the bottom of the pan with buttered brown paper or foil.

Basic Baked Fish

one 3 to 4 lb. fish, dressed
1/4 cup melted butter or margarine
salt and pepper to taste

Place fish in buttered baking dish. Sprinkle inside and out with salt and pepper. Bake at 425° to 450°F. for 10 minutes per inch of thickness (see the Canadian Rule, page 14). Baste twice during baking time with drippings. Makes 4 to 6 servings.

BROILING

Thick pieces of fish are best for broiling. Fillets don't work well because they dry out during the broiling process. You may marinate fish prior to broiling. Remember, lean fish must be basted often. For very thin fish, broil two inches from the heat source. For thick fish, broil four to six inches from heat source.

Basic Broiled Fish

2 lbs. fish steaks
2 tbs. melted butter **or** oil
2 tbs. lemon juice

1 tsp. salt
1/2 tsp. paprika
dash pepper

Place steaks in a single layer on a preheated and oiled broiler pan. Combine remaining ingredients. Pour over fish. Broil 4 to 6 minutes. Turn. Baste with sauce. Broil the additional minutes necessary to total 10 minutes per inch of thickness (see the Canadian Rule, page 14).

OVEN FRYING

Once known as baking at a high temperature, this method is now called oven frying. It is a favorite because it renders a crisp fish without the odor, calories or clean-up of deep fat frying. It is faster than baking and very easy. The best pieces to use are whole fish, dressed, fillets, or steaks. You do not have to turn the fish with this method of cooking.

Basic Oven Fried Fish

2 lbs. fish fillets
1 tbs. salt
1 cup milk

1 cup dry bread crumbs **or** cracker crumbs
1/4 cup melted butter **or** margarine

Cut fillets into serving size portions. Add salt to milk. Dip fillets into milk, then into crumbs. Place in a single layer in a buttered baking dish. Drizzle butter evenly over fillets. Bake at 500°F. for 10 minutes per inch of thickness (see the Canadian Rule, page 14). Baste lean fish after 5 minutes. Makes 4 to 6 servings.

PAN FRYING

Small whole fish, fillets and frozen fish portions or sticks are best prepared this way. Use oil in combination with butter to help prevent butter from burning. Fish prepared by pan frying will be crisp on the outside, tender and juicy on the inside.

Basic Pan Fried Fish

2 lbs. fillets, steaks or pan dressed fish
salt and pepper to taste
1 egg, beaten
1 tbs. milk

1 cup dry bread crumbs, cracker crumbs, cornmeal **or** flour
1/4 cup **each** butter and oil

Cut fillets into serving size pieces. Sprinkle both sides with salt and pepper. Add milk to egg, beat well. Dip fish in milk mixture. Roll in crumbs. Melt butter with oil in large frying pan. Fry fish over moderate heat until brown on one side. Turn, brown on other side. Fry a total of 10 minutes per inch of thickness (see Canadian Rule, page 14). Drain on absorbent paper. Makes 4 servings.

DEEP FAT FRYING

Small fish fillets are best for this method. Before you dip the fish in batter, it must be completely dry, or the batter will not stick. Use a deep fat fryer, wok or deep, heavy pan. Fill it only half full with vegetable oil. Make sure you use only fresh oil. The oil must be hot enough, usually 375°F., or the fish will be greasy. It is wise to use a thermometer. Cook only a few pieces of fish at a time, so that temperature of oil will not drop. Keep cooked pieces in a warm oven while frying the remaining pieces.

Basic Deep Fat Fried Fish

1/3 lb. small fish fillets, per serving
any fritter batter
vegetable **or** peanut oil, enough to half fill the pan
Mustard Sauce, page 148 (optional)

Cut fish into smalll pieces. Dry them well. Dip in batter. Fry in oil heated to 375°F. 10 minutes per inch of thickness (see the Canadian Rule, page 14). If desired, serve with Mustard Sauce.

POACHING

This method works with any type of fish. It is best, however, with whole, lean fish. Flavorful fish, such as salmon and red snapper, can be poached in lightly salted water. The flavor of mild fish is enhanced with the addition of herbs and spices to the poaching liquid. Some flavorful broths in which fish can be poached are Court Bouillon (page 135) and Fish Stock (page 134). Unless you are using a fish poacher, wrap the fish in cheesecloth and lower it into simmering liquid which just covers the fish. Wait until the poaching liquid returns to simmer, then cook 10 minutes per inch of thickness (see the Canadian Rule, page 14). The cheesecloth will allow you to easily remove the fish intact from the liquid when it is done. Reserve the poaching broth for soups, sauces, or any recipe calling for fish stock.

Basic Poached Fish

2 lbs. fish fillets or steaks
cheesecloth (if not using fish poacher)
water or broth (see above)

salt
herbs and spices (optional)

Wrap fish in cheesecloth (if not using fish poacher). Place fish in single layer in poacher or large pan. Add enough liquid just to cover fish. Add salt and seasoning. Bring to a boil over medium heat. Turn down heat to a low simmer. Cook 10 minutes per inch of thickness (see above). Makes 4 to 6 servings.

FISH FAMILIES

If you find a recipe you'd like to try, but the fish called for is unavailable, read over the chart beginning on page 22 for some alternatives. By comparing the descriptions of Fish Families, you should be able to find acceptable substitutes. The major factor to keep in mind is fat content. If your recipe calls for a lean fish, such as bass, substitute another lean fish, such as cod or perch. If an oily fish is called for, like catfish, substitute another oily fish, like mackerel. (See Fat Content of Fish, page 2.)

When you become proficient in your understanding of fish, you may wish to interchange oily and lean fish. Remember, however, that a lean fish requires frequent basting.

If you have a fish of unknown fat content, check the flesh color. White, or very light colored fish is lean. Dark colored flesh indicates a high oil content. Tan, or light brown flesh indicates moderately fatty fish.

Fish Families	Flavor, Texture, Fat Content and Hints	Species
Bass	Mild flavor, Firm flesh. Low fat content. Remove leathery skin before cooking.	black bass, blackfish, black jewfish, black sea bass, crappie, giant sea bass, grouper, white sea bass, snook, striped bass, yellow bass, white perch
Bluefish	Depends upon where fish feeds. If Gulf Coast, sweet flavor, moderate fat content. If East Coast, strong flavor, high oil content.	blue snapper, fatback, skipjack, snapping mackerel, tailor
Carp	Moderately strong flavor. Best in winter months. Firm flesh. Moderate fat content. Best cooked simply.	Bohemian/French, Israeli

Fish Families	Flavor, Texture, Fat Content and Hints	Species
Catfish	Delicate flavor. Firm, yet flaky. Moderate fat content. Remove leathery skin before eating. Good pan fried.	blue catfish, brown catfish, channel catfish, flat bullhead, gafftopsail, green bullhead, sea catfish, spotted catfish, walking catfish
Cod	Mild flavor. Tender flesh. Very low fat content.	Atlantic cod, burbot, codfish, cusk, hake, haddock, Pacific cod, pollock, poor cod, scrod, tomcod
Drum	Mild flavor. Tender flesh. Low fat content.	barbed drum, big drum, channel bass, croaker, drumfish, gray drum, sheepshead, striped drum white perch, whiting

Fish Families	Flavor, Texture, Fat Content and Hints	Species
Flounder	Mild, distinctive flavor. Tender, flaky flesh. Broiling not recommended because of low fat content. 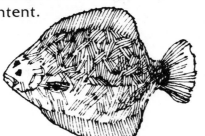	American plaice, Atlantic halibut, arrowtooth, California halibut, fluke, Pacific halibut, sanddab, Southern flounder, starry flounder, turbot, windowpane
Mackerel	Rich, sometimes strong flavor. Firm flesh. High fat content. Before cooking remove dark lateral line of accumulated carbohydrates to avoid bitter taste.	American mackerel, Atlantic mackerel, bluefin, blue mackerel, bonita, Boston mackerel, Pacific mackerel, Spanish mackerel, tuna (albacore), yellowfin

Fish Families	Flavor, Texture, Fat Content and Hints	Species
Mullet	Mild flavor. Tender flesh. Moderate fat content.	black mullet, jumping mullet, liza, sand mullet, silver mullet, striped mullet, white mullet
Perch	Mild flavor. Tender, flaky flesh. Very low fat content. Small fish best pan fried.	blue pike, red perch, redfish, sauger, walleye, yellow perch, yellow pike
Pike	Mild flavor. Very bony. Low fat content. Difficult to scale. Pour boiling water over skin to ease job.	Muskelunge, northern pike, walleye
Pompano	Rich, distinctive flavor. Firm flesh. Moderate fat content.	great pompano, permit, golden pompano, Carolina permi, cobblerfish, butterfish

Fish Families	Flavor, Texture, Fat Content and Hints	Species
Porgy/Scup	Mild flavor. Coarse grain. Low fat content. Best prepared simply. Large fish have better flavor and fewer bones.	grass porgy, jolthead, Pacific porgy, porgy, scup, white bone
Rockfish	Mild flavor. Low fat content. Firm flesh.	rock cod, Pacific red snapper, grouper, Pacific Ocean perch
Salmon	Rich, distinctive flavor. Firm, yet flaky flesh of light pink to red color. The more red the flesh, the richer the taste.	Atlantic salmon, chinook salmon, chum salmon, coho salmon, humpback salmon, keta salmon, king salmon, pink salmon, red salmon, spring salmon, silver salmon, silverside salmon, sockeye salmon

Fish Families	Flavor, Texture, Fat Content and Hints	Species
Shark	Distinctive flavor, like swordfish. Very firm, meat-like flesh. Soak in saltwater or milk before cooking to neutralize strong flavor. No bones. Tough cartilage.	blue shark, bull shark, dogfish shark, grayfish shark, greyfish shark, leopard shark, mako shark, pinback shark, tiger shark, thresher shark
Smelt	Rich flavor. Firm, yet tender flesh. Bony, best pan fried.	candlelight fish, frostfish, icefish, whitebait
Sole	Mild, disinctive flavor. Tender, flaky flesh. Very low fat content.	butter sole, curlfin sole, Dover sole, English sole, lemon sole, petrale sole, rex sole, rock sole, sand sole

Fish Families	Flavor, Texture, Fat Content and Hints	Species
Sturgeon	Strong flavor, like swordfish and shark. Firm, dry flesh. Low fat content.	green sturgeon, white sturgeon
Swordfish	Strong flavor, like sturgeon and shark. Firm, meatlike flesh. Moderate fat content. When cooking, needs frequent basting.	broadbill
Tilefish	Mild flavor. Firm, yet tender flesh. Compares to scallops in texture. Low fat content.	blackline tilefish, ocean tilefish, sand tilefish
Trout	Mild, yet distinctive flavor. Firm flesh. Moderate fat content.	brook trout, brown trout, cutthroat trout, Dolly Varden trout, golden trout, lake trout, rainbow trout

Clams Casino (page 55) ▶

SHELLFISH

Shellfish, the most popular of all seafood, are lean, nutritious and easily digested. Coupled with the fact that they are also high in minerals, they are a boon to dieters and health conscious people alike.

ABALONE

The only place in the United States where abalone are found is in the coastal waters of California. From the warm tides of Southern Baja to the cold waters of the California/Oregon border, divers search for these succulent mollusks. They can usually be found clinging to the underside of a large rock.

Although you can only enjoy fresh abalone in California (because abalone faces extinction, and is not allowed to be sold outside of California), frozen and canned abalone from Mexico and Japan are available at most markets.

The edible part of the abalone, the muscle, or "foot," is housed in a 5 to 9-inch oval shell. The inside of the shell is the renowned mother-of-pearl.

To prepare the abalone, detach it from the shell. Remove and discard the entrails.

◄ Seviche (page 59)

Trim and discard black flesh along rim of abalone. Wash the abalone thoroughly. What you now have is a creamy white "hat-shaped" object. To make the abalone really tender, place it on a firm, flat surface and whack it quite hard with a large flat board (a 2 x 8-inch piece of lumber is ideal). The preceding step is not essential, but will facilitate the tenderizing, or pounding. After slicing abalone horizontially as thin as possible, you must pound the pieces until they are soft to touch and much larger in diameter. Don't leave any hard spots within the slice.

To pan fry: Dip abalone slices into beaten eggs. Roll slices in flour, seasoned to taste with salt and pepper (preferably white). Heat 1/4-inch of vegetable oil in a heavy skillet until very hot but not smoking. Fry abalone slices about 30 seconds on each side, or until golden. Do not overcook, or abalone will toughen. Drain slices on paper towels. Serve immediately. One medium-size abalone should serve about 4 people.

CLAMS

Clams are burrowing bivalve mollusks found off both east and west coasts. Although there is a difference in varieties most are interchangeable in recipes. East coast clams are the hard shell clams called little necks (smallest), cherrystones (mid size) or quahogs (largest). Also found on the east coast are soft-shell (or long-necked), so called because of their thin, brittle shells. West coast clams are butter, razor, large Pismo and very large geoduck clams (up to 1-1/2 pounds each).

When you purchase clams live, tap their shell. They should close tightly. Discard any that do not.

Whether you buy them or dig them yourself, all clams need to be scrubbed with a stiff brush before cooking. Also, remove the hair-like substance, known as beard, that hangs from the shell.

If you have dug them yourself, they need to be purged to get rid of the sand. To purge, soak clams in a mixture of one gallon of water, one cup of salt and one cup of cornmeal for several hours. Keep them in a cool place while purging.

To shuck, hold a scrubbed clam in your hand with the hinge against the palm. Insert a narrow, sharp knife between the shells. Cut around the edge to release the muscle. Twist and pry open.

MUSSELS

Mussels are bivalve mollusks that attach themselves to rocks in the inter-tidal zone and feed on plankton. The flesh is tender and has a distinctive, smoky taste. Mussel meat is bright orange when cooked. They are harvested commercially on the Atlantic Coast and can be gathered by individuals on the Pacific Coast except in the months during the mussel quarantine, usually May through August. Always check with the Fish and Game Department to see if they are safe to eat before gathering them. You will need a fishing license.

To clean mussels simply scrub shells with a stiff brush under running water and cut off the whiskers that protrude from the shell. You can keep them 1 or 2 days in the refrigerator before cooking. Discard any that have opened and will not close when tapped.

SQUID

Squid is a cephalopod mollusk—an elongated, ten-armed cousin of the octopus. Calamari is its Italian and most popular name. Its body includes a flesh-body pouch, long tentacles and edible fins.

To clean a squid you first rinse in cold water and remove the shell-like pen. (It is this pen which makes it a part of the shellfish family.) Pull back the rim of the body pouch to locate the edge of the pen and pull the pen free of the surrounding flesh. Discard the pen. Pull the body and head gently apart. The viscera (intestines) including the ink sac should come out with the head and tentacles. Take the pouch and pull off the irregularly patterned skin, do the same to the fins. Remove the tentacles from the head by cutting just below the eyes. Discard the head and viscera. Within the flesh that holds the tentacles together is a bony beak or mouth. With your fingers squeeze out the beak and discard.

You now have four pieces of completely edible squid flesh; the pouch, the tentacles and the two finds. Squid is delicious deep fried and in salads.

Frozen squid that has been thawed should be used immediately, fresh squid can be stored, well-wrapped in the refrigerator for one day.

CRABS

There are many varieties of crab, and most are interchangeable in recipes. The favorites of the west coast are the Alaskan King crab (from six to twenty pounds), which inhabits the waters of the Pacific Northwest; and the Dungeness crab (one to three pounds), found from Alaska to Mexico. A popular crab of the Atlantic and Gulf Coasts is the Blue crab (which is also the soft-shelled crab while molting). It can weigh from one quarter to one pound while "hard" and from two ounces to one-third pound while "soft." Another common crab in this area is the Rock crab. It is small and averages only one-third of a pound in weight.

Crabs must be alive when they are cooked. The meat must be cooked before it is removed from the shell.

To boil crab: In large kettle, bring about eight quarts of water and two tablespoons of salt to boil. Wash crab thoroughly in cool water. Immerse two or three at a time in boiling water. Boil Blue crabs 8 minutes per pound. Dungenness crab takes only 20 minutes altogether.

To open crab: You may wish to protect your hands by wearing rubber gloves or a potholder glove. Twist and break off all claws and legs.

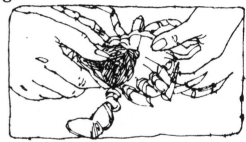

For Blue crabs, lift up skirt and break it off.

Force upper shell off. It may be necessary to use a knife.

Separate the shell from the body.

Remove and discard spongy material, gills, intestines and sandbags.

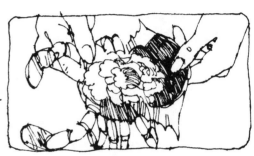

Pull meat apart.

Break claws with nutcracker or mallet to loosen meat.

LOBSTERS

This may well be the most popular of all shellfish. There are two varieties of lobster. The ones from New England are the largest and most delicious, and their exceptionally large claws are very meaty. The small Pacific, or rock lobsters are found on the southwest coast of the United States. The meat of this lobster however, is found exclusively in the tail. Their claws contain almost no meat.

Like crab, lobster should be purchased alive.

To boil live lobster: In a large kettle, boil enough water, plus one tablespoon of salt per quart of water, to cover the lobster. Pick up lobster behind large, front claws. Plunge, head first, into boiling water. Cover the kettle. A one pound lobster takes about 7 minutes to cook. 10 minutes should be ample for a two pound lobster. A hint: Small lobsters are the most tender. Remove lobster when done, and submerge in cold water to stop cooking process. Rinse and drain.

To clean and serve boiled lobster: Using a sharp, heavy knife, cut the lobster lengthwise from head to tail. Split it completely in two.

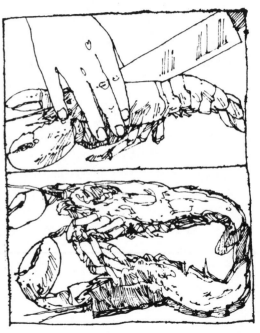

Holding lobster open, remove and discard stomach and intestinal vein. The liver (or tomalley) and Coral are considered to be delicacies. You may remove them and serve them with the lobster, or throw them away.

As soon as you have cleaned the lobster, serve it. My family likes it best with lots of melted butter and lemon juice. The Coral is delicious mixed with butter. Use about 1/4 to 1/2-cup of soft butter and mash it with the Coral from one lobster. Then spread on lobster meat.

To eat claws, crack them with a nutcracker or smash them with a mallet. Pick out meat with a small fork.

Another fine way to prepare lobster is to broil it.

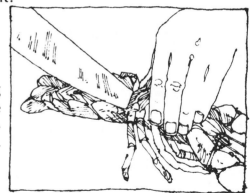

To broil lobster: To kill a lobster for broiling steady the lobster right side up. With a sharp knife tip pierce the shell and flesh at center of the cross-shaped mark behind the head. This severs the spinal cord and painlessly kills the lobster.

Next, cut the lobster in half lengthwise.

Remove and discard stomach and intestinal vein. Remove Coral and liver and reserve or discard.

Crack the claws.

Preheat broiler pan. Place lobster flesh side up on broiler pan. Brush shell and meat with butter.

Put lobster in oven four inches from the heat source. Broil 10 to 12 minutes, depending upon the size of the lobster, or cook until lightly browned. Serve immediately with more melted butter and lemon juice. Pick out meat from tail and claws with a small fork.

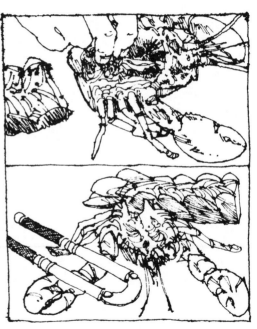

CRAYFISH

A crustacean related to the lobster, but much smaller. It is also known as the crawfish, crawdad, ecrevisse or mudbug. Crayfish can be found almost everywhere. They inhabit quiet streams, ponds, rivers, lakes, creeks and canals. You'll find them moving lazily around a depth of from one to ten feet. You can catch your own by hand, or buy them at your local market.

To prepare a crayfish to cook: Crayfish are sold alive and are cooked in their shells. They have an intestinal vein that most cooks like to remove. Some remove it before cooking, others remove it after cooking and some don't remove it at all. To remove before cooking, hold the crayfish steady right side up and then lift the center tail flap and twist to free it. Then pull the tail flap away from the body to remove the intestinal vein. Alternately you can throw the live crayfish into boiling, salted

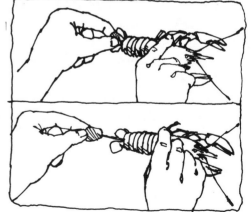

water for 1 minute to kill it, then take it out of the water, remove the tail flap and vein and then continue cooking it.

To boil: Prepare crayfish to cook (see above). Bring enough water to boil to cover crayfish while they cook, plus commercial type crab boil, 2 tablespoons pickling spices or onions, parsley and red wine. Plunge crayfish in head first and boil about 8 minutes, or until they turn bright red. Cover pot tightly while they boil.

To bake: Prepare crayfish to cook (see above). Place in preheated 400°F. oven, on a baking dish, for 15 to 20 minutes, or until lightly browned. Baste them frequently, as they have a tendency to dry out.

To eat: Pull tail away from body. Crack claws. Pick out meat from tail and claws with a small fork. Serve with plain melted butter and lemon juice.

Because of their small size eating crayfish is a messy process. So, wear a bib and dig right in.

SHRIMP AND PRAWNS

These tasty little morsels are popular everywhere. They are available in just about every size from small to jumbo. Prawns are larger than shrimp and in spite of a slight difference in flavor and texture, they are interchangeable.

Both may be cooked with or without their shells. Purists feel that they retain a better flavor when they are left in their shells.

To shell and devein: Pull off and discard tiny legs. A long slender device, available in the housewares department of most stores, will enable you to shell and devein in one quick stroke. If you don't have one of these, simply peel off skin. You may leave on, or pull off, tail. Remove the sand vein by cutting along the top side of the shrimp with a small knife or your finger.

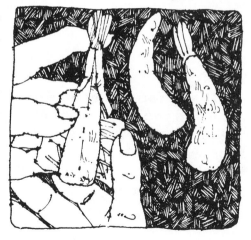

Rinse under cold water.

To butterfly: After deveining, make a deep cut along the back, cutting almost, but not completely, through the body.

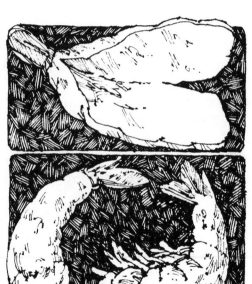

To cook shrimp or prawns: Bring one quart of water and two tablespoons of salt to a boil. Drop in one to two pounds of shelled or unshelled shrimp or prawns. Turn down heat. Simmer for 3 minutes. Be carefull not to overcook. As soon as they turn pink, they are done.

Open Faced Fish Sandwich (page 80) ▶

OYSTERS

These fine mollusks are found on both the east and west coasts. They are sold live in the shell or shucked. Make sure when you buy them in the shell that they close tightly when you tap their shell. Oysters that do not close tightly when tapped are dead and inedible. Some of the more popular varieties include blue point, from the east, and Pacific Coast or Olympia variety. Small oysters have a mild flavor. The large, Pacific Coast oysters have a strong flavor.

To clean and shell: Scrub oysters with a stiff brush and run under cold water. To open oyster, you may wish to "bill" it first. To do this, hammer off a small section of the flat shell, not the round, at the unhinged edge. This will make it easier to shuck.

◄ Landlubber's Chowder (page 132)

Next force a thin, yet sturdy knife into the hinge of the shells. It is best to wear gloves as you do this. Turn the knife to pry and lift the upper shell enough to cut through the hinge muscle. Then run knife between the shells to open.

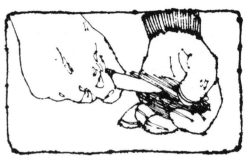

If you are serving the oysters raw, "on the half shell," discard the flat shell. Serve the oyster on the round shell, arranged in a bed of rock salt.

If you prefer oysters slightly cooked, poaching is a good method. Many recipes call for this preparation, rather than for raw oysters.

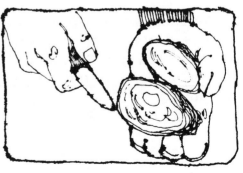

To poach oysters: Bring two cups of water and one half teaspoon of salt to a boil in a frying pan. Add one cup of shucked oysters. Lower heat, and simmer 4 to 6 minutes. Do not overcook. Oysters are done when their edges begin to curl and they appear "plump."

APPETIZERS

Both fish and shellfish make delicious appetizers. No matter what you are planning for the rest of the meal, they offer a refreshing change.

I have divided the appetizers into two groups; those which are served as dips, spreads and finger foods to go with cocktails, and those, such as Steamers, Clams Casino, Moules Mariniere and Seviche, which are served at the table as a first course. Most of the recipes are relatively inexpensive and many can be made ahead. The spectacular results you receive from these recipes belie their ease of preparation.

 # BAKED CRAB SPREAD

Simplicity and elegance combine for this party-time favorite.

1 cup crab
1 cup low calorie mayonnaise
1 cup cheddar cheese, shredded
1/2 cup onion, finely chopped
1 tsp. cream style horseradish sauce, or to taste
dash of Worcestershire sauce

Pick over the crab to remove all cartilage. Mix all ingredients in an oven-proof casserole. Bake uncovered at 375° for 20 minutes or until golden brown. Serve hot with an assortment of crackers or vegetables. This recipe is easily doubled. Makes 3-1/2 cups.

 # MINI SHRIMP QUICHES

This has all the qualities of a party recipe: good, easy, may be frozen.

1 pkg. refrigerated butterflake rolls
1/2 lb. bay shrimp, cooked
1 egg, beaten
1/2 cup light cream
1 tbs. brandy
1/2 tsp. salt
dash pepper
1-1/2 ozs. Gruyere or Swiss Cheese

Grease twenty-four 1-3/4″ muffin pans. Separate each roll in half and press into pans to form shells. Place one or two shrimp in each. Combine egg, cream, brandy, salt and pepper. Slice cheese into 24 pieces. Place one piece in each shell. Cover with egg mixture. Bake at 375° for 20 minutes. Serve cool or wrap to freeze. If frozen, bake 10-12 minutes at 375°. Makes 24 servings.

 # SHRIMP PUFFS

These melt-in-your-mouth morsels will disappear quickly. Luckily for the busy hostess, they can be prepared several hours in advance and popped into the oven at the last minute.

1 sheet frozen puff pastry
1/4 lb. cooked bay shrimp
4 ozs. ricotta cheese
1 egg, slightly beaten

2 tsp. lemon juice
1 green onion, finely chopped
1/2 cup cheddar cheese, shredded

Defrost pastry sheet as directed on box. Meanwhile, combine ricotta cheese, egg, lemon juice, green onion and cheese. Roll pastry sheet to a 12"x12" square, using a small amount of flour if necessary to prevent sticking. Cut into 2" squares. Top each square with a teaspoon of filling. Brush two edges of each square with milk, and fold to make a triangle. Press edges together. Place on an ungreased baking sheet. Chill until ready to bake. Preheat oven to 450°. Place pan in oven, reduce heat to 400°, and bake 12-15 minutes until light golden brown. Makes 36 appetizers.

 # SHRIMP TOAST

You don't need to serve Chinese food to enjoy this tasty appetizer or luncheon dish. It is a good make-ahead recipe that can be frozen after frying and reheated in the oven just before serving.

6 slices day-old bread
1/2 lb. medium raw shrimp
1/4 cup water chestnuts, finely chopped
2 green onions with tops, chopped
1 tbs. cornstarch
1 tbs. dry sherry

1 small egg, beaten
1/2 tsp. fresh gingerroot, minced
1/2 tsp. salt
sesame seeds
vegetable oil

Remove crusts from bread. Air dry two hours before using. Shell, devein and chop shrimp. Mix remaining ingredients except sesame seeds and oil. Spread on bread, packing it on to make it stick. Press seeds on top. Cut bread from corner to corner to make 24 triangles. Pour oil in a wok or pan to 1″ depth and heat to 370°. Fry a few pieces at a time. Start with filling side down for 1-2 minutes; turn for 1 minute until golden. Drain on paper towels. Keep warm in a 200° oven if serving very soon, or cool, wrap and freeze. Reheat at 400° about 10 minutes if frozen. Makes 24 appetizers.

 # TUNA ST. JACQUES

Vary this with cooked fresh or canned crab or tuna, or use leftover fish.

2 (6-1/2 ozs. each) tuna, packed in water
1 tbs. olive oil
4 green onions with tops, sliced
1/4 lb. mushrooms, finely chopped
1 can cream of mushroom soup

1/2 cup dry vermouth or chicken broth
3 tbs. Parmesan cheese
1/4 cup dried bread crumbs
2 tbs. butter or margarine, melted

Drain and flake tuna. Heat oil in a frying pan and saute onions and mushrooms. Stir in soup and vermouth. Bring to a simmer. Butter 6 scallop shells (available in kitchen shops or import stores) or 6 individual ramekins. Divide half of sauce among shells. Top each with tuna. Spoon remaining sauce over tuna. Mix Parmesan cheese and bread crumbs and sprinkle over tops. Drizzle with melted butter. Heat in a 425° oven for about 10 minutes until browned on top and heated through. Makes 6 servings.

 **TROUT PATE**

When trout is on your menu, cook extra so you can prepare this in minutes.

1 large or 2 small trout, cooked
2 hard-boiled eggs, chopped
1 tbs. lemon juice
3 tbs. dry white wine
1/2 tsp. pepper

1/2 tsp. dill weed
salt to taste
8 ozs. cream cheese, softened
3 tbs. pistachio nuts, chopped
crackers or melba toast

Remove skin and bones from trout. You should have at least one cup cooked fish. In a blender or food processor, mix trout, eggs, lemon juice, wine, pepper, dill weed and salt. Add cream cheese and blend thoroughly. Press into a crock, mold or small bowl. Chill well. Top with nuts just before serving. Serve with crackers or melba toast. Makes approximately 2 cups.

Variation: Other stronger fish, such as salmon, swordfish or tilefish, may be used; but substitute cognac or brandy for the white wine.

 # MOULES MARINIERE

This is an adaption of a French recipe. It tastes much like clams Bordelaise.

2 quarts mussels
1/4 cup butter
1/2 cup chopped green onion
3 cloves garlic, minced
pinch of thyme

1 bay leaf
1/4 tsp. white pepper
1 cup dry white wine
2 tbs. chopped parsley
French bread (optional)

Scrub mussels well. Melt butter in Dutch oven type pan or large kettle. Add onions and garlic. Saute 5 minutes. Add thyme, bay leaf, pepper, wine and mussels. Cover tightly. Shake pan a few times to distribute liquid. Simmer about 8 minutes, or until most of the mussels are open. Discard any mussels that are not open. Place mussels in individual soup bowls. Spoon wine mixture over mussels. Sprinkle with parsley. Serve with French bread. Makes 4 servings.

 **CLAMS CASINO**

1 dozen cherrystone clams
rock salt, enough to fill ovenproof baking
    dish in which you cook clams
3 slices bacon, diced
1/3 cup **each** finely chopped onion and celery
1/4 cup finely chopped green pepper

1 tbs. lemon juice
1 tsp. seasoned salt
1/4 tsp. **each** pepper
    and Worcestershire sauce
1 tbs. catsup
1/4 tsp. seafood seasoning

Scrub clams well. Place in large frying pan with water 1 inch deep. Cover and bring to boil. Simmer about 3 minutes, just until clams begin to open. When clams are cool enough to handle, break off half the shell. With a small knife, pull clam away from shell, but do not remove it from shell. Arrange clams on rock salt in baking dish, or in baking dish without rock salt. Fry bacon a few minutes, until it has rendered some of its fat. Add onion, celery and green pepper. Saute mixture until vegetables are cooked. Add remaining ingredients. Heat. Spoon mixture over clams. Bake at 400°F. for 4 to 5 minutes, just until the edges of the clams begin to curl. Do not overcook, or the clams will toughen. Makes 4 to 6 servings.

 # CRAB AND CHUTNEY DELUXE

This savory combination could not be easier to prepare.

1 pkg. (8 ozs.) cream cheese
1/4 cup chutney

1 can (5 ozs.) crab meat, drained
crisp unsalted crackers

Place cream cheese on serving plate. Spread chutney over top. Arrange crab on chutney. Serve with crackers. Makes about 18 servings.

 # SCALLOP WHIRLS

24 scallops, defrosted if frozen
12 strips bacon

wooden toothpicks

Pat scallops dry with paper towel. Cut bacon strips in half. Wrap a half-strip of bacon around each scallop. Secure with a toothpick. Broil 6 inches from heat source about 3 to 4 minutes until bacon is crisp and scallop tender. Makes 24 pieces.

 **OLIVE OYSTER DIP**

1 can (6.6 ozs.) smoked oysters
1 pkg. (8 ozs.) cream cheese, softened
1/2 cup minced ripe olives

1 tsp. lemon juice
1/8 tsp. garlic salt

Drain oysters reserving liquid. Chop. Add oyster liquor to cream cheese and blend well. Carefully blend in remaining ingredients, including oysters. Serve with crisp crackers. Makes about 1-1/2 cups.

 **SHRIMP DIP**

2 cans (6 ozs. each) shrimp
3 tbs. catsup
3 tbs. dry sherry

2 tbs. horseradish
1 pkg. (8 ozs.) cream cheese, softened

Rinse the shrimp in cold water and drain well. Mix with remaining ingredients. Chill a few hours to blend flavors. Serve with your favorite thin crackers or vegetables. Makes about 2 cups.

 **MARINATED SHRIMP**

These shrimp develop an agreeable tart flavor after marinating.

2 lbs. fresh, raw shrimp
2 medium onions, thinly sliced
1-1/2 cups vegetable oil
1-1/2 cups white vinegar
1/2 cup sugar
1-1/2 tsp. **each** salt and celery seed
4 tbs. capers with juice

Peel and devein shrimp (see page 43). Bring one quart of water and two tablespoons of salt to a boil. Simmer shrimp in water for about three minutes, or until they turn pink. Drain. Rinse in cold water to stop cooking process. Chill. When cold, alternate layers of shrimp and onion rings in a sealable container. Mix remaining ingredients. Pour over shrimp. Seal container. Refrigerate for six hours or more. Shake container every hour or so. Remove shrimp from marinade. Arrange attractively on serving platter. Makes about 18 servings.

 **SEVICHE**

This raw fish appetizer is very popular in Japan and certain South American countries. The lime juice in which it marinates actually firms the fish and turns it opaque. Serve as a first course on lettuce leaves in cocktail cups or in a wide bowl at cocktail time for help yourself service.

1 lb. fresh white fish (red snapper,
   blackfish, flounder or turbot)
1 cup fresh lime juice
1 ripe tomato, diced
1/4 cup sliced green onion

1 can (4 ozs.) diced green chiles
   or sliced stuffed green olives
1/4 tsp. ground oregano
salt and pepper to taste
cilantro or parsley, chopped (optional)

Cut fish into small cubes. Arrange in a single layer in a glass dish. Add remaining ingredients, except cilantro. Stir well. Cover and chill for at least 6 hours, or until fish turns completely white. Serve garnished with cilantro. Makes 10 to 12 servings.

MAIN DISHES

Seafood offers more variety and greater nutrition than beef, yet only in the last few years has the general public become aware of its value. The current emphasis on "keeping fit" and health foods has finally brought seafood into the limelight.

Fish, and especially shellfish, have significantly fewer calories and fat than beef. For example, a three ounce hamburger patty has about 316 calories and 26 grams of fat, while three ounces of salmon, which is considered an "oily" or rich fish, contains about 140 calories and 7.1 grams of fat. An even more striking example is crabmeat. It has about 89 calories and 2.5 grams of fat.

Eating salmon or crab for dinner might allow a weightwatcher to splurge on dessert. Seafood is also recommended for people on low carbohydrate diets.

Whether you're on a special diet, or simply enjoy the adventure of delicious, healthy eating, seafood entrees may be just what you need to spark your appetite at dinner time.

Coquilles St. Jacques (page 96) ▶

GREEK BAKED FISH

4 lbs. dressed fish (flounder, sea bass, cod)
salt and freshly ground pepper
juice of 1 lemon
1/4 cup olive oil
2 large onions, thinly sliced
3 medium tomatoes, sliced

2 tbs. parsley, minced
12 black Greek olives
1/2 cup dry white wine
1 tbs. bread crumbs
1 lemon, sliced

Sprinkle fish with salt, pepper and lemon juice. Brush a baking pan with olive oil. Place a layer of onions and a layer of tomatoes on the bottom of pan. Place fish on top; layer with remaining onions, tomatoes, parsley and olives. Add wine to remaining olive oil and pour over fish. Sprinkle crumbs on top, cover and bake in a 350° oven for 45 minutes or until fish is barely firm, basting occasionally with sauce. Uncover, top with lemon slices and serve. Makes 6 servings.

◀ Seafood Mousse (page 144)

 # BAKED FISH ALFREDO

This is an all-purpose recipe that can be used with any fresh fillets or steaks.

2 lbs. sole, rock cod, red snapper or other fillets
2 tbs. A-1 sauce
2 tbs. lemon juice
2 tbs. oil
1/2 tsp. garlic powder
salt and pepper to taste

Arrange fillets in a baking dish. Mix remaining ingredients and pour over fish. Bake at 375° for approximately 20 minutes, less if fish is very thin. Sprinkle with paprika. Serve with any favorite sauce or lemon wedges. Makes 4-5 servings.

 # HALIBUT WITH DILL PICKLE SAUCE

The unusual topping will complement any white fish steaks you choose.

2 lbs. halibut steaks, 1″ thick
1 cup plain yogurt or sour cream
6 green onions, minced
1/2 green pepper, diced
4 tbs. dill pickle, diced
2 tbs. parsley, minced
2 tbs. lemon juice
1/2 tsp. dry mustard
1/2 tsp. sweet basil
1/2 tsp. salt
1/2 tsp. pepper

Arrange halibut in a 9″x13″ baking pan. Mix remaining ingredients and spread over steaks. Bake at 350° for 30 minutes. Makes 6 servings.

 # GRILLED AHI (TUNA) WITH PINEAPPLE SALSA

For extra special flavor, try the newest California idea in grilling. Add a handful of moistened grapevines (preferably chardonnay) to your charcoal or gas grill. Other local chips such as mesquite may be used instead.

4 ahi (yellowfin tuna) steaks, 1″ thick
Dijon type mustard
1/2 cup seasoned rice vinegar (available in Japanese grocery)
1/2 tsp. fresh gingerroot, grated

Spread steaks liberally with mustard. Place in a sealable plastic bag. Add rice vinegar and gingerroot to bag and marinate fish 1 hour, turning frequently. Heat broiler or grill. Place steaks on grill 4″ from heat source. Cook 4-5 minutes per side. Serve with **Pineapple Salsa**, page 65. Makes 4 servings.

Variations: Use halibut, mahimahi, swordfish, mako shark, tilefish or grouper.

 # PINEAPPLE SALSA

1/2 medium pineapple, peeled, cored
1/2 cup red pepper, cut in 1/4" dice
4 medium green onions with tops, sliced
1 tsp. fresh gingerroot, minced
1 serrano chili, seeded and minced, or 2 tsp. canned green chilies
    plus 1/2 tsp. red pepper flakes
1 tbs. lemon or lime juice
dash salt

Cut pineapple into 1/4" dice, reserving juice. Add pineapple, juice and all remaining ingredients. Stir. Allow to blend for several hours or up to 3 days. Serve at room temperature.
See **Sauces**, page 146, for other fruit salsas.

 # WISCONSIN FISH BOIL

The early Scandanavian settlers of Door County, Penninsula, the "thumb" of Wisconsin, are credited with originating this delightful feast. You can duplicate the irresistible flavors of this popular event. The meal is traditionally completed with a tangy coleslaw, several varieties of bread, including light rye, and cherry pie.

6 fresh or frozen fish steaks cut 1-inch thick
18 small red potatoes in jackets
12 small boiling onions
1 cup salt (yes, this is the correct amount)

1/2 cup butter, melted
2 tbs. chopped parsley (optional)
6 lemon wedges (optional)

Thaw fish if frozen. Fill an 8-quart kettle, which has a basket (similar to a deep fry basket), about 2/3 full of water and heat to a rapid boil. Wash potatoes and remove any deep eyes. Skin onions. When water is boiling rapidly, add salt. The cooked food will not taste too salty. Put potatoes and onions in basket. Boil hard for 18 minutes. Carefully add steaks. Continue to boil rapidly for 12 more minutes. Test with a long fork to be sure the fish and potatoes are cooked. Remove from water and drain. Divide fish, potatoes and onions among six heated plates. Pour melted butter over all. Sprinkle with parsley. Serve with lemon wedges. Makes 6 servings.

BLACKFISH WITH SPINACH MUSHROOM STUFFING

Absolutely terrific! That's what my family said the first time they tasted this recipe. Although the blackfish is generally a sport fish, it is sometimes found in East Coast markets. Cape Cod to the Delaware Bay is the normal habitat of the blackfish, which is also known as the "tautog."

one 4 to 5 pound blackfish, bass or flounder, dressed
salt and pepper
1/2 pkg. frozen chopped spinach, defrosted and drained
1/2 cup sliced, fresh mushrooms

wooden toothpicks
1/4 cup butter, melted
2 tbs. lemon juice

Line a shallow baking dish, with foil. Grease foil. Cut off head and tail, if you have not already done so. Rinse and pat dry. Sprinkle cavity with salt and pepper. Put spinach in cavity and spread with mushrooms. Secure fish closed with toothpicks. Mix together butter and lemon juice. Pour over fish. Using a ruler, measure thickest part of fish. Cook fish 10 minutes per inch of thickness (see Canadian Rule, page 14). Bake at 400°F. Baste with pan juices when half cooking time is over. This fish does not separate into the "flakes" that most of the others do. Makes 4 to 5 servings.

SEAFOOD MANICOTTI

This is a delicious way to serve manicotti, and a good choice if you are having guests.

1 lb. mixed seafood, shellfish and fillets
1 tbs. olive oil
3 cloves garlic, minced
1 (15 ozs.) can marinara sauce
1 (6 ozs.) can tomato paste
1 (14-1/2 ozs.) can peeled, diced tomatoes
1 cup water
2 tsp. basil
1 tsp. oregano

1 tbs. parsley, chopped
salt and pepper to taste
8 ozs. lowfat ricotta cheese
1/2 cup lowfat cottage cheese
1/2 cup Parmesan cheese, grated
2 eggs, slightly beaten
14 manicotti noodles, uncooked
grated Parmesan cheese

Saute seafood briefly in olive oil and remove with a slotted spoon. Add garlic, marinara sauce, tomato paste, diced tomatoes including juice, water, basil, oregano, parsley, salt and pepper to oil. Simmer 30 minutes. Combine ricotta, cottage cheese and 1/2 cup Parmesan cheese. Fold in seafood. Grease a 9"x13" pan. Dip each manicotti noodle briefly in water, fill with cheese-seafood mixture and place in pan. Pour sauce over manicotti and cover pan tightly with foil. Bake at 350° for 45 minutes, remove from oven, sprinkle with more Parmesan cheese and return to oven for 5 minutes. Remove and let sit for 15 minutes before serving. Makes 6-7 servings.

 # MAHIMAHI TERIYAKI

Mahimahi (or dolphinfish) is a favorite of everyone dining in Hawaii. The flesh is firm when cooked, and the flavor is sweet and delicate. It is more readily available fresh than in the past but is often found frozen. Substitute any firm white fish for this easy lowfat recipe.

2 lbs. mahimahi or other firm fish fillets
1 cup teriyaki sauce
2 tbs. dry sherry
1 tbs. sesame seeds

Place fillets in a plastic bag or container with a tight lid. Combine teriyaki sauce, sherry and sesame seeds. Pour over fillets. Marinate an hour or more, turning container frequently. Broil 5″ from heat about 10 minutes per inch of thickness, turning after 5 minutes. Baste occasionally. This is also excellent for the barbecue. Makes 6 servings.

 # BAKED FISH IN WHITE WINE

3 to 3-1/2 lbs. any firm white fish
1/2 medium onion, sliced
3 shallots, minced
1 cup sliced mushrooms
1 tbs. lemon juice
salt and pepper to taste
pinch **each** nutmeg and cloves

dry white wine
2 tbs. brandy
2 tbs. flour
2 tbs. soft butter
dash cayenne
parsley (optional)
lemon slices (optional)

Dry fish with paper towels. Butter a large baking dish and arrange fish in it. Separate onions into rings. Scatter over fish. Combine shallots, mushrooms, lemon juice, salt, pepper, nutmeg and cloves. Sprinkle over fish and onions. Almost cover the fish with wine. Bake at 425°F. 10 minutes per inch of thickness (see Canadian Rule, page 14). Remove from oven. With a baster, remove all cooking liquid to a small saucepan. Reduce liquid over high heat to 1-1/4 cups. Warm brandy in a ladle. Light it carefully. Pour flaming brandy into reduced liquid. Set aside. Cream together flour and butter. Add to liquid. Stir mixture constantly over medium heat. When thick, add cayenne and pour over fish. Garnish with parsley and lemons. Makes 8 servings.

 # STEAMED OPAKAPAKA WITH VEGETABLES

Opakapaka is the Hawaiian name for pink snapper. Red snapper works equally well.

2 lbs. opakapaka or red snapper fillets
salt
1 tsp. fresh gingerroot, minced
1 clove garlic, minced
2 cups Chinese cabbage (won bok), shredded

4 green onions with tops, sliced
1 tomato, sliced
1/2 bunch watercress, chopped
1/4 cup sesame oil
4 tbs. soy sauce

Place fillets on a steamer rack and sprinkle with salt, minced ginger and minced garlic. Place over simmering water and cover. Steam for 15-20 minutes until cooked. To serve, arrange one cup of Chinese cabbage on a platter. Place fish on top. Arrange remaining cabbage, onions, tomato and watercress on fish. Heat sesame oil until very hot. Add soy sauce and immediately pour over fish and vegetables. Makes 6 servings.

 # SOLE ALMANDINE

1 lb. fillet of sole
4 tbs. butter
1/4 cup sliced almonds
1/3 cup flour
1/2 tsp. salt
dash pepper
1 tbs. lemon juice
1 tbs. finely chopped parsley

Pat fillets dry with paper towel. Melt 2 tablespoons butter in a small skillet. Saute almonds until lightly browned. Set aside. Season flour with salt and pepper. Dredge fillets in seasoned flour. Melt remaining 2 tablespoons butter in large skillet over medium-high heat. Add fillets and fry about 2 to 3 minutes or until the first side is golden brown. Turn and fry the additional minutes necessary to total 10 minutes per inch of thickness (see Canadian Rule, page 14). Remove fillets to a heated ovenproof platter and place in warm oven. Return almonds to heat. Add lemon juice and stir until mixture boils. Spoon over fillets. Sprinkle with parsley. Makes 4 servings.

 # BROILED FILLETS WITH TANGERINE SAUCE

1 lb. firm white fish fillets
1 tbs. butter or margarine, melted
1 tbs. tangerine or orange juice
salt and pepper

Thaw fillets if frozen. Place in a single layer in a well-greased baking pan. Combine melted butter with juice. Brush over fish. Sprinkle with salt and pepper. Broil fish 10 minutes per inch of thickness (see Canadian Rule, page 14). Baste once during broiling with pan juices. Arrange fish on a warm serving platter. Serve with Tangerine Sauce. Makes 2 to 4 servings.

Tangerine Sauce—Saute 1/4 cup sliced almonds in 2 tablespoons butter. Mix 1 tablespoon cornstarch with 1/2 cup tangerine or orange juice in a 1-quart saucepan. Add 2 tablespoons **each** white wine, apple jelly and lemon juice. Cook, stirring, until mixture thickens. Add a dash of hot pepper sauce, pinch of salt, 1/2 teaspoon grated tangerine or orange rind, 1 tangerine or orange, peeled and cut into small pieces, and the sauteed almonds and butter. Heat and serve with broiled fillets. Makes 1 cup.

 # FILLETS IN PARCHMENT

Parchment is available in large grocery stores and kitchen shops. If unavailable, use foil. The wrapping holds in all the juices. Cut four 15″ squares.

1-1/2 lbs. fish fillets or steaks, 1″ thick
1 carrot, peeled, cut into matchsticks
1 tomato, chopped
1 zucchini, cut into matchsticks
4 mushrooms, sliced
1/2 onion, sliced

Fold each parchment paper in half and cut as you would make a Valentine. Place fish near fold line. Cover with vegetable layers, beginning with carrot matchsticks and ending with onion slices. If desired, drizzle with a little sesame oil. Starting at the point, fold edges of parchment over twice to enclose fish and vegetables. Place in a low-sided pan and bake

at 450° until packet is puffed and golden. Fillets need 8-10 minutes; steaks need 15 minutes. Put each packet on a dinner plate. Cut open, but do not remove paper. Makes 4 servings.

 # CRUSTY FILLETS WITH SWEET-SOUR SAUCE

1 lb. sole, flounder or other thin fillets
1 cup fine buttery cracker crumbs
1/2 cup flaked coconut
1 egg, beaten

1 tbs. evaporated milk
1/4 tsp. salt
1/4 cup cooking oil
Sweet-Sour Sauce

Thaw fish if frozen. Cut in serving size portions. Mix cracker crumbs and coconut. Combine eggs, milk and salt. Dip fish in egg mixture. Shake off excess and coat well with cracker-coconut mixture. Heat 2 to 3 tablespoons oil in a 12-inch frypan. Fry fillets, a few at a time, over moderate heat for 10 minutes per inch of thickness (see page 14). Turn fillets only once. Drain on paper towels and place in warm oven while frying remaining fillets. Serve with Sweet-Sour Sauce. Makes 2 to 3 servings.

Sweet-Sour Sauce — Combine 1/2 cup apricot or plum preserves, 1/4 cup **each** catsup and light corn syrup, 2 tablespoons lemon juice and 1/4 teaspoon ginger in a small saucepan. Simmer over low heat 2 to 3 minutes. Serve with coconut-crusted sole. Makes about 1 cup sauce.

 # SOLE SURPRISES

1-1/2 to 2 lbs. sole fillets (8 pieces)
1/4 lb. small shrimp, cooked, shelled
    and deveined (see page 43)
1/4 cup fine dry bread crumbs
1/2 tsp. fines herbes
1/4 tsp. onion salt

1/4 tsp. dill
1/4 cup grated Parmesan cheese
3 tbs. mayonnaise
1 can cream of mushroom soup, undiluted
2 tbs. dry sherry
chopped chives, for garnish (optional)

Dry fish with paper towels. Grease 4 six-ounce Pyrex custard cups. Arrange two pieces of fish in an "X" pattern in the cups. Make sure to have the fillets touching the sides and bottom of the cups. Fillets will overlap and hang out the sides of the cups quite a bit. Stir together shrimp, bread crumbs, fines herbes, onion salt, dill, Parmesan cheese and mayonnaise. Divide mixture among fillets and stuff. Fold excess fish over filling, completely enclosing the filling. Bake at 350°F. for 30 to 40 minutes. Just before fish is done, heat soup and sherry together in a saucepan. When fish is done, turn cups upside down on a serving platter. Spoon sauce over fillets. If desired, sprinkle with chives. Makes 4 servings.

◀ Crayfish (page 41)

 # BAKED TILEFISH WITH TOMATO SAUCE

Tile is a marvelous fish that is caught in very deep, mid-Atlantic waters. If this is not available in your area, choose any firm, mild flavored fish such as flounder or sole.

1-1/2 lbs. tilefish, flounder or sole
1 can (8 ozs.) tomato sauce
1/2 cup finely chopped onion
1/2 tsp. Bon Appetit seasoning (Schilling)
1 tbs. oil
2 tbs. fresh lemon juice

Grease a baking dish. Arrange fillets in a single layer. Mix remaining ingredients. Pour over fish. Bake at 425°F. for 10 minutes per inch of thickness (see Canadian Rule, page 14). Makes 4 servings.

 **SHRIMP STUFFED TILEFISH**

If you cannot find tilefish, you may substitute any member of the flatfish family.

1-1/2 lbs. tilefish, butterfly cut (see page 5)
1/4 lb. fresh shrimp, deveined
1/2 cup grated Havarti **or** Swiss cheese
1/4 cup sliced green onions, including tops
1/2 tsp. salt
1/2 tsp. dill

2 tbs. mayonnaise
wooden toothpicks
2 tbs. butter, melted
3 tbs. lemon juice
1 lemon, sliced (optional)
parsley sprigs (optional)

If you cannot find butterfly cut, slice the thick fillets almost all the way through.
Arrange fish in a greased, glass baking dish. Mix the shrimp, cheese, onions, salt, dill and mayonnaise together. Divide mixture among fillets and stuff. Secure closed with wooden toothpicks, only if needed. Mix butter and lemon juice together. Pour over fillets. Bake at 425°F. for 10 minutes per inch of thickness (see Canadian Rule, page 14). If desired, garnish with lemon slices and parsley. Makes 4 servings.

 # OPEN FACED FISH SANDWICH

Serve this good tasting favorite with a vegetable soup or fruit salad for a complete meal.

2 cups leftover fish, or 2 cans, 6-1/2 ozs. each, tuna
1/4 cup finely chopped celery (optional)
2 tbs. Tartar Sauce, page 147
1/2 tsp. dillweed
salt and pepper to taste
2 large tomatoes
8 slices bread, toasted
1 cup grated mild cheese

Skin, flake and debone fish. Add celery, if desired. Blend in enough tartar sauce to bind mixture together. Season with dill, salt and pepper. Thinly slice the tomatoes and dry each side on paper towels. Arrange on toast. Spread with fish mixture. Sprinkle cheese on top. Broil four inches from heat source about 3 minutes, until cheese bubbles. Makes 4 servings.

 # TURBOT PARMESAN

Turbot is a delicate flatfish which can be used in any flounder or sole recipe.

1-1/2 lbs. turbot fillets (or any flatfish)
1/2 tsp. salt
pepper to taste
3/4 cup sour cream
1/2 cup grated Parmesan cheese
1 tbs. chives
1/4 cup fine dry bread crumbs
paprika
watercress (optional)

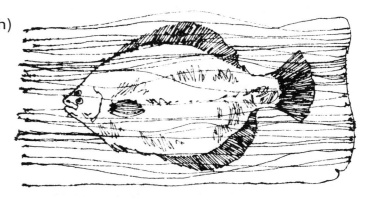

Wash and pat turbot dry with paper towels. Arrange in greased baking pan. Sprinkle salt and pepper over fish. Mix sour cream with cheese, chives and crumbs. Spread over fish. Dust with paprika. Bake at 450°F. for 10 minutes per inch of thickness (see Canadian Rule, page 14). Garnish with watercress. Makes 4 servings.

# GOURMET FLATFISH

A classic **duxelle** mixture, which consists of mushrooms, onions and herbs, bakes beneath any fish from the flatfish family.

1 tbs. salad oil
1 tbs. flour
1/4 cup finely chopped mushrooms
1/3 cup finely chopped onions
3/4 tsp. crushed tarragon leaves
1/4 cup dry white wine, **or** fish stock
1/4 cup cream **or** milk

2 lbs. flatfish fillets (such as turbot, dab, fluke or sole), skins removed
salt, pepper and paprika to taste
1/4 cup dry bread crumbs
2 tbs. melted butter
1 cup shredded, mild cheese

Pour oil into a 13 x 9 x 2-inch baking dish. Stir in flour. Sprinkle mushrooms, onions and tarragon over flour. Stir in wine and cream. Dry fillets with paper towels. Place them over **duxelles** mixture. Combine salt, pepper, paprika and bread crumbs. Sprinkle over fish. Pour melted butter over crumbs. Bake at 425°F. for 10 minutes per inch of thickness (see Canadian Rule, page 14). Add cheese the last 5 minutes of baking. Makes 4 to 5 servings.

TUNA ELEGANTE

Your family won't groan when you tell them you're serving this tuna casserole for dinner.

2 cans (6-1/2 ozs. each) tuna, drained
1 pkg. (10 ozs.) frozen asparagus, defrosted
   or 1 bunch fresh asparagus
1 can mushroom soup, undiluted
3 cups cooked rice
1 pint cottage cheese

2 tbs. grated onion
1/2 cup sour cream
1/4 cup sliced black olives
2 tbs. butter, melted
1/2 cup bread crumbs

Drain and flake tuna. Reserve six asparagus spears. Cut remainder into 1/4-inch pieces. Mix tuna, asparagus, soup, rice, cottage cheese, onion, sour cream and olives. Pour into greased two quart casserole. Add bread crumbs to melted butter and sprinkle over top. Bake at 350°F. for 30 to 35 minutes. During last 10 minutes of baking time, steam asparagus spears. When casserole is done, garnish with asparagus. Makes 6 servings.

 # TUNA TOFU PATTIES

1/2 cup dried mushrooms
1 cake firm tofu
1 (6-1/2 ozs. each) cans tuna, drained
2 eggs

1 green onion, finely chopped
1/2 tsp. salt
2 tbs. soy sauce
1 small carrot, grated

Soak mushrooms in water until soft and chop finely. Squeeze excess water from tofu and crumble. Add to mushrooms with remaining ingredients and mix well. Drop by spoonfuls onto a lightly greased hot frying pan. Flip patties when golden. Serve with your favorite sauce or fruit salsa. Makes 4 servings.

 **SPICY COD BAKE**

Cod is popular and abundant throughout the world.

1 lb. cod fillets
1/2 lb. mushrooms
2 carrots
1 medium-sized onion
salt and pepper

juice of 1/2 lemon
1 cup V-8 or tomato juice
1/4 tsp. dry mustard
1 tsp. vinegar
1 tsp. Worcestershire sauce

Rinse cod and pat dry with paper towels. Chop mushrooms, carrots and onion finely. To make this job easy, use a food processor. Spread half of this mixture in a greased baking dish. Arrange fillets in a single layer on top. Sprinkle with salt and pepper. Squeeze lemon juice over the fish. Spread remaining vegetable mixture on top of fish. Mix V-8, mustard, vinegar and Worcestershire sauce. Pour over the fish. Bake at 425°F. 10 minutes per inch of thickness (see Canadian Rule, page 14). Makes 4 servings.

 # BAKED HAKE TARRAGON

Hake is similar to cod, and may be substituted in any recipe calling for cod. It is almost fat free, tasty and sweet.

1-1/2 lbs. hake fillets (or cod, haddock, burbot, ling, pollock, scrod)
salt and pepper to taste
3 tbs. butter, melted
1/2 tsp. fresh tarragon, **or** 1/4 tsp. dried tarragon, crushed
1/4 tsp. Bon Appetit seasoning (Schilling)
paprika
parsley (optional)
lemon wedges (optional)

Dry fillets with paper towel. Place in single layer in a shallow, greased baking dish. Sprinkle with salt and pepper. Combine butter, tarragon and Bon Appetit. Pour over fish. Sprinkle with paprika. Bake at 425°F. 10 minutes per inch of thickness (see Canadian Rule, page 14). Garnish with parsley and lemon wedges. Makes 4 servings.

 # WILD AND WONDERFUL STUFFED TROUT

The deceptively rich taste belies the healthy ingredients in this recipe.

4 medium-to-large trout, dressed
1/2 cup green onions with tops, sliced
1 cup mushrooms, halved and sliced
1 tbs. extra-light olive oil
1 cup cooked wild rice,
    or white and wild mix

1 tbs. dry sherry or vermouth
salt and freshly ground pepper
1 tsp. parsley, chopped
zest (peel) of 1 lemon
juice of 1 lemon

Open slit in trout as far as possible. Working fingers from tail toward head, loosen bones from flesh. Gently pull out (scissors help). Make stuffing: slice onions and mushrooms and saute in hot olive oil. Stir in rice, sherry, salt and pepper. Remove from heat, add parsley and lemon zest and set aside to cool. Heat oven to 400°. Cover low-sided pan or cookie sheet with foil and spray with vegetable oil spray. Place trout on foil skin side down. Cut lemon and squeeze over fish. Divide rice mixture and fold fish to close. Push together to hold stuffing in, arranging trout on its side. Brush skin with oil. Bake at 400° for 10-12 minutes until flesh is opaque. Makes 4 servings.

 # NORTHWOODS MUSKIE

The largest of the pike family, the muskellunge is found in fresh water lakes throughout the area of the Great Lakes, and sometimes in the Pacific Ocean near Alaska. This easy recipe is the favorite of a champion muskie catcher.

4 to 6 fillets of muskellunge (or any member of the pike family,
    see chart beginning on page 22)
salt and pepper to taste
1/4 cup butter, melted
light cream, enough to cover fish

Arrange fillets in a single layer in a greased baking dish. Salt and pepper to taste. Pour melted butter and cream over fish. Bake at 425°F. 10 minutes per inch of thickness (see Canadian Rule, page 14). Makes 4 to 6 servings.

 # STUFFED TOMATOES AU GRATIN

When your garden blesses you with an abundance of giant tomatoes, try this recipe. Any leftover canned or smoked fish may be used.

6 large, ripe tomatoes
salt
2 cups cooked fish, flaked
1 cup cooked rice
3/4 cup grated Swiss cheese
1 egg, beaten
1/2 tsp. oregano
1 tbs. butter, melted
1/4 cup dried bread crumbs

Remove cores and hollow out tomatoes. Sprinkle with salt. Turn over on paper towels. Drain for 15 minutes. Mix fish with rice, cheese, egg and oregano. Fill tomatoes with mixture. Place in greased baking dish. Mix together butter and crumbs. Sprinkle over tomatoes. Bake at 350°F. for 15 minutes. Makes 6 servings.

# GRILLED SWORDFISH STEAK

The mayonnaise "melts" into the swordfish after cooking, but you'll notice the succulence it lends to the fish.

1 swordfish steak per person (each 3/4 to 1-inch thick)
mayonnaise
lemon butter: For 4 servings, 1/4 cup melted butter and juice of 1 lemon
chopped parsley (optional)

If cooking outside, on a grill, start fire and allow to burn for 20 to 30 minutes. The coals must be very hot. If cooking indoors, preheat broiler. Spread a generous portion of mayonnaise on one side of each steak. If cooking outside, place mayonnaise side down on grill. If cooking inside, place mayonnaise side up, closest to heating element. Broil about 6 minutes. Turn and spread mayonnaise on other side. Broil steaks enough additional minutes to equal 10 minutes per inch of thickness (see Canadian Rule, page 14). Prepare lemon butter. Arrange steaks attractively on serving platter. Garnish with parsley. Serve with lemon butter.

 # BROILED MAHIMAHI

Only rarely is Mahimahi available anywhere except on the West Coast and in Hawaii. Substitute with any other fish steaks.

1 - 1/2 lbs. mahimahi steaks
3 tbs. butter **or** margarine
1 clove garlic, minced
1 tsp. soy sauce
2 tbs. lemon juice
1 tbs. minced parsley (optional)

Pat steaks dry with paper towels. Place in greased baking dish in single layer. Melt butter. Add garlic and saute until limp. Remove from heat. Stir in soy sauce and lemon juice. Pour over steaks and allow to marinate at least 15 minutes, longer if desired. Broil four inches from heat, turning once, until fish just begins to flake. Cooking time should be 10 minutes per inch of thickness (see Canadian Rule, page 14) or about 4 to 5 minutes on each side depending upon thickness of steaks. Garnish with parsley. Makes 4 servings.

 # BROILED SALMON STEAKS

Any fish steaks, about 1″ thick, are suitable for this treatment.

6 medium salmon steaks
1/3 cup olive oil
1/2 cup parsley, chopped
1/2 tsp. dill weed
1 tsp. salt
4 cloves garlic, crushed

1 cup fine dry bread crumbs
1 tbs. butter or margarine
1-1/2 tbs. olive oil
6 large slices tomato
fresh parsley

Place salmon on a well-greased broiler pan. Combine 1/3 cup olive oil, parsley, dill weed, salt, garlic and bread crumbs. Mix well and set aside. Melt butter, stir in 1-1/2 tbs. olive oil, and brush half over salmon steaks. Broil 4″ from heat for 4 minutes. Turn and brush with remaining butter-oil mixture. Broil 4 minutes longer or until fish barely begins to flake. Cover with tomato slices. Pack bread mixture on top and broil until lightly browned, about 1-2 minutes. Makes 6 servings.

Broiled Salmon Steaks (see variation page 92) ▶

 **SALMON DIVINE**

Remember this method to remove bones from any fish that has all the bones growing from a central backbone (some fish have two sets of ribs).

1 whole salmon
4 tbs. butter or margarine, melted
2-3 drops liquid smoke
1/2 tsp. garlic powder
1 tbs. lemon juice
freshly grated Parmesan cheese

Split salmon entirely in order to lay flat on a broiler pan. Scissors are handy for this. Broil 5″ below heat source about 10 minutes, until backbone and ribs can be removed in one piece. **Hint:** pull from head to tail. Meanwhile, add liquid smoke, garlic powder and lemon juice to melted butter and stir. Spread sauce over fish, covering entire surface. Liberally sprinkle Parmesan cheese over fish. Bake at 375° for 25-30 minutes until fish flakes easily. Makes 6-8 servings.

◄ Broiled Fillets with Tangerine Sauce (page 73)

# FORGOTTEN SALMON

Be sure the fish you use has the skin attached on one side. You need a grill with a cover such as the Weber kettle. No peeking allowed for perfect results.

1 large salmon, filleted and butterflied (2-3 servings per lb.)
1/4 lb. butter or margarine
1/4 cup dry white wine
2 tbs. soy sauce
1 large onion, sliced
garlic salt or garlic powder

With two layers of aluminum foil 6″ longer than the length of the salmon, make a pan that has 2″ turned up on all four sides. Melt butter over low heat. Add wine and soy sauce. Place pan over hot coals on a grill with a cover. Pour butter sauce in pan. Lay fish on butter, arrange onions over fish and sprinkle with garlic salt or powder. Cover and cook for 30 minutes. It is not necessary to peek or baste for perfectly cooked fish.

LINGUINE WITH CLAM SAUCE

Absolutely spectacular with fresh clams and homemade noodles.

1/4 cup butter
3 cloves garlic, minced
1/2 cup heavy cream
salt and pepper to taste
20 to 24 fresh, clams, steamed and shucked (see page 31), with liquor reserved,
    or 1 can (8 ozs.) clams
linguine noodles to serve 4
1/2 cup grated Parmesan cheese

Melt butter in saucepan over medium-low heat. Add garlic. Saute for 5 to 8 minutes. Watch carefully, so that butter does not burn. Add cream, salt, pepper and reserved clam liquor. Keep mixture warm over low heat. Boil noodles until done. Drain. Add clams to cream mixture. Heat until just warm. Divide noodles among plates. Top with clam sauce. Sprinkle with cheese. Makes 4 servings.

COQUILLES ST. JACQUES

1-1/2 lbs. fresh or frozen scallops
3/4 cup dry white wine **or** chicken broth
1 bay leaf
1/2 tsp. salt
1-1/2 cups thinly sliced fresh mushrooms
2 tbs. green onion
1/4 cup butter

6 tbs. flour
dash white pepper
1/4 tsp. nutmeg
1 cup light cream
2 tbs. butter, melted
1 cup soft bread crumbs

Thaw scallops, if frozen. Place in saucepan with wine and bay leaf. Simmer about 2 minutes, until scallops turn white. Remove scallops. Pour wine poaching liquid from saucepan into measuring cup. Add enough broth to liquid to bring the two up to the one cup mark. Saute mushrooms and onions in 1/4 cup butter until tender. Stir in flour, pepper and nutmeg. Blend until flour is absorbed. Add reserved poaching liquid and cream. Stir until thick. Add scallops. Warm over low heat. Do not boil, or mixture will curdle and scallops will toughen. Butter 6 baking shells, ramekins, or custard cups (6 ozs.). Divide mixture evenly among containers and fill. Add bread crumbs to remaining 2 tablespoons of butter. Sprinkle over top of scallop mixture. Bake at 400°F. about 5 to 7 minutes, until lightly browned.

HERB FRIED SCALLOPS

Crisp on the outside, tender in the middle. These delicate morsels will melt in your mouth.

1 lb. ocean scallops
2 eggs
1 tbs. lemon juice
1 cup fine dry bread crumbs
1/2 tsp. dried herbs (thyme, tarragon, dill and parsley)
vegetable oil
Tartar Sauce

Clean and rinse scallops. Cut large ones in half. Dry completely on paper towels. Beat eggs well. Add lemon juice. Mix your choice of herbs with bread crumbs. Dip scallops in crumbs, in egg mixture, then in crumbs again. Heat 1/4-inch of oil in frying pan. Fry coated scallops about 3 minutes on each side, until golden. Drain on paper towels. Serve immediately with Tartar Sauce. Makes 4 servings.

SCALLOPS IN WHITE WINE

This classic preparation results in a simple yet elegant dish.

1-1/2 lbs. sea scallops, shucked
6 tbs. butter
salt and pepper to taste
3 shallots, finely chopped
2 tbs. fresh parsley, chopped
1/2 cup white wine

Cut the sea scallops into 2-3 slices. Place in a non-aluminum saucepan. Add remaining ingredients. Bring to a simmer over medium heat, cover and cook for 3-5 minutes, until scallops are opaque. Remove scallops with a slotted spoon, increase heat and boil sauce for 5 minutes, reducing original volume by half. Return scallops to pan and heat through. Serve immediately. Makes 6 servings.

SCALLOPS WITH LEMON PASTA

Calorie-wise but loaded with flavor, this is sure to be a family favorite.

1 lb. bay scallops
1 cup white wine
1 cup water
2 tbs. lemon juice

1/2 lb. linguine, fettucine or
    angel hair pasta
1/2 cup Parmesan cheese, freshly grated
1 tbs. fresh parsley, chopped

Pasta sauce:
3/4 cup reduced-calorie sour cream
3/4 cup lowfat cottage cheese

zest (peel) of two lemons
2 tbs. lemon juice
cayenne pepper to taste

Rinse scallops. Combine wine, water and lemon juice in a small pan. Heat to simmering. Add scallops and simmer just until scallops turn white. Drain and set aside to cool. Cook pasta in boiling water for 8 minutes or until al dente. Meanwhile, prepare sauce: place ingredients in a food processor or blender container, process briefly and transfer to a nonstick pan. Heat gently over low heat for about 2 minutes. Drain pasta and toss with sauce, Parmesan cheese and parsley. Serve immediately. Makes 4 servings.

SEAFOOD LASAGNA

To reduce the fat and calories, substitute lowfat ricotta for the cream cheese and use lowfat cottage cheese. Replace the American cheese with more Parmesan cheese.

8 lasagna noodles
1 cup onions, chopped
2 tbs. butter
8 ozs. cream cheese, softened
1-1/2 cups cream style cottage cheese
1 egg, beaten
2 tbs. dried basil
salt and pepper to taste

2 cans cream of mushroom soup
1/3 cup milk
1/3 cup dry white wine
1 lb. cooked baby shrimp
1/2 lb. fresh crab or 1 (6 ozs.) can
1/4 cup Parmesan cheese, grated
1/2 cup sharp American cheese,
    shredded

Cook lasagna noodles according to package directions. Drain well. Arrange 4 noodles in a 9"x13" baking dish. In a large saucepan, cook onions in butter until tender. Blend in cream cheese; stir in cottage cheese, eggs, basil, salt and pepper. Spread half of the cheese sauce on noodles. Combine soup, milk and wine. Stir in shrimp and crab. Spread half over

cheese sauce. Repeat the layers. Sprinkle with Parmesan cheese. Bake uncovered at 350°
for 45 minutes. Top with American cheese. Bake 3-5 minutes more. Let stand for 15 minutes
before serving. Makes 12 servings.

SEAFOOD SUPREME IN A PASTA RING

A mixture of seafood complements angel hair pasta in this party-perfect dish.

1/2 lb. mushrooms, sliced
1 medium green pepper, diced
1 medium red pepper, diced
1 large onion, coarsely chopped
2 cloves garlic, minced
2 tbs. extra-light olive oil
2 cups broccoli flowerets

1-1/2 cups dry white wine
2 tbs. flour
1 (12 ozs.) can evaporated skim milk
1 can tomato paste
1/2 tsp. pepper
1 lb. bay scallops
1 lb. medium shrimp, shelled, deveined

In a Dutch oven, cook mushrooms, peppers, onion and garlic in olive oil until just tender. Add broccoli. Blend wine and flour and add to pan; cook, stirring until thickened and smooth. Blend in skim milk, tomato paste and pepper. Add scallops and shrimp and cook, covered, for 10 minutes over low heat until fish is cooked. Spoon fish and sauce into center of Pasta Ring (recipe follows), spooning some sauce over pasta. Serve immediately. Makes 8 servings.

PASTA RING

4 cups hot cooked angel hair pasta (8 ozs. uncooked)
1/2 cup Parmesan cheese, freshly grated
1/4 cup Italian parsley, chopped
2 tbs. olive oil

In a bowl blend pasta, cheese, parsley and olive oil. Press into an oiled 4-cup ring mold. Unmold onto a serving plate.

PAELLA

A spectacular dish to serve company. Traditionally served in a Paellero, a large, round, shallow dish about fifteen inches in diameter which can be purchased at a cookware store. Or, you may substitute any large, shallow oven-proof dish.

1/4 cup olive oil
6 **each,** chicken drumsticks and thighs
3 whole chicken breasts, split into 4 pieces each
1/2 lb. chorizo or hot Italian sausage, cut into 2-inch chunks
2 cups long grain rice
3/4 cup sliced green onion, with green tops
4 cloves garlic, minced
2 stalks celery, chopped
1 green pepper, seeded and chopped
1 tsp. saffron
1 tsp. salt
1 tsp. oregano
4 cups chicken stock

Paella continued

1 can (15 ozs.) artichoke hearts, halved
20 large fresh shrimp, shelled and deveined (see page 43)
20 fresh clams, in their shells, well scrubbed

Heat olive oil in frying pan over medium-high heat. Add chicken pieces, and brown thoroughly. Remove chicken and drain well on paper towels. Add chorizo, brown well. Remove and drain on paper towels. Drain all but 1/4-cup of fat. Add rice, onion, garlic, celery and green pepper. Saute over medium heat, until rice is golden and vegetables are somewhat soft. Add saffron, salt, oregano, stock and artichoke hearts. Simmer for five minutes. Pour rice mixture into one or more large, shallow baking dishes. Rice should be no closer than one inch to the top of the dish. Arrange chicken pieces attractively on top of the rice. Cover, with lid or aluminum foil, and bake at 350°F. for 20 minutes. Arrange raw shrimp and clams on top of rice mixture. Cover and bake for an additional 8 minutes. Makes 8 to 10 servings.

CRAB-SPINACH COTTAGE BAKE

Have some leftover fish? Substitute one cup of flaked, cooked fish for the crabmeat in this recipe.

1 can (7 ozs.) crabmeat
1 pkg. (10 ozs.) frozen spinach, defrosted and well drained
1/4 tsp. nutmeg
1 cup cottage cheese
1/3 cup finely chopped onion
1/2 cup grated cheese (such as Provolone, Monterey Jack, Muenster)
1/2 cup tomato juice
1 tsp. Worcestershire sauce
1 tbs. lemon juice

Drain and pick over crab. Combine spinach and nutmeg. Spread in a small, greased casserole. Combine cottage cheese, onion and cheese. Spoon over spinach. Top with crabmeat. Combine remaining ingredients. Pour over crab. Bake at 350°F. for 20 minutes. Makes 4 servings.

CRAB NEWBURG

This is a delicious way to use leftover lobster, shrimp, crab or scallops.

4 tbs. butter
2 cups diced, cooked crab, lobster, shrimp, scallops
1/4 cup dry sherry
1/2 tsp. paprika
dash of nutmeg
3 egg yolks, beaten
1 cup cream or milk
salt and white pepper to taste
4 large puff pastry shells (from your grocer's frozen foods department),
   or 8 slices toast, buttered

In top of double boiler, melt butter. Stir in the crab. Cook until warm, about 3 minutes. Add sherry. Cook 2 minutes. Add paprika and nutmeg. Over medium heat, add egg yolks and cream. Stir constantly until thickened. Add salt and pepper. Fill pastry shells, or serve over toast. Makes 4 servings.

MARYLAND CRAB CAKES

Maryland, home of the delicious Blue Crab, offers us these delicacies.

1 lb. crabmeat
1 cup Italian seasoned breadcrumbs
1 egg, beaten
1/4 cup mayonnaise
1/2 tsp. salt
1/4 tsp. pepper
1 tsp. Worcestershire sauce
1 tsp. dry mustard
margarine, butter **or** oil

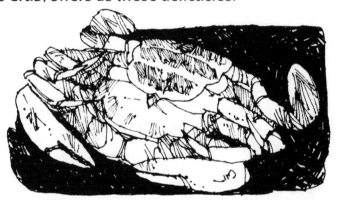

Remove cartilage from crabmeat. Mix breadcrumbs, egg, mayonnaise and seasonings, except margarine. Add crab. Mix gently but thoroughly. Shape into 6 cakes. Fry in skillet on medium-high heat, in just enough fat to prevent sticking. Cook until browned, about 5 minutes per side. Makes 6 cakes.

Glazed Shrimp Kabobs (see page 114) ▶

SHRIMP WITH HOT SAUCE

A friend who is originally from Hong Kong shares this tasty Chinese treat.

1 lb. fresh shrimp or prawns
1 egg white
1 tsp. sherry
1 tsp. salt
1-1/2 tsp. cornstarch
3/4 cup vegetable oil
1 tbs. garlic, chopped
2 tbs. green onions with tops, chopped

2 tbs. tomato catsup
1 tsp. chili paste or chili oil
1/2 tsp. sugar
1/2 tsp. salt
3 tbs. soup stock or water
2 tsp. cornstarch
1 tsp. sesame oil

Peel and devein shrimp and pat dry. Mix egg white, sherry, salt and cornstarch. Add shrimp and marinate 30 minutes. Add oil to wok and heat. When hot, add shrimp and stir-fry until 90% cooked. Drain shrimp and set aside, reserving 2 tbs. oil. Return oil to wok. Heat again, adding garlic and onions. Toss to cook. Meanwhile mix catsup, chili paste, sugar, salt, stock, cornstarch and sesame oil. Add to wok with shrimp, and cook just long enough to heat shrimp through. Serve immediately. Makes 4 servings.

◀ Shrimp and Rice (page 115)

BARBECUED SHRIMP, TEXAS STYLE

This is a recipe for a crowd, but it can easily be cut down to suit your needs.

8 lbs. fresh large shrimp or prawns
1 cup olive oil
3 tbs. Worcestershire sauce
2 lemons, sliced
3 tbs. parsley, chopped
2-3 tbs. liquid smoke
3 tbs. oregano

1/2 lb. butter
8 ozs. chili sauce
4 cloves garlic, chopped
2 tsp. paprika
1 tsp. Tabasco sauce
salt and pepper to taste

Wash deheaded shrimp and remove all shell except tail. Arrange in a shallow pan. Combine remaining ingredients in a saucepan, heating over low heat until butter is melted and everything is well combined. Pour over shrimp. Marinate overnight or for at least two hours. Bake at 300° for 30 minutes, turning every 10 minutes. Makes 15-20 servings.

CRAB OR SHRIMP "SOUFFLE"

2 cups fresh, flaked crabmeat, **or**
2 cups small, fresh shrimp, shelled
and deveined (see page 43)
1 cup mayonnaise
1/2 cup **each** finely chopped celery
and onion
1 medium green pepper, chopped
2 tbs. minced parsley

1 tsp. **each** grated lemon peel and salt
1/4 tsp. pepper
8 to 10 slices bread
4 eggs
3 cups milk
1 can mushroom soup, undiluted
1 cup fresh, cooked mushrooms, sliced
1/4 cup grated Parmesan cheese

In a large bowl, combine the crab, mayonnaise, onion, celery, green pepper, parsley, lemon peel, salt and pepper. Cut four slices bread into 1-inch cubes. Place in bottom of greased 3-quart rectangular casserole. Spoon crab mixture over bread cubes. Remove crusts from remaining bread. Fit slices to completely cover crab mixture. Beat eggs slightly. Add milk. Pour over bread. Cover and refrigerate overnight. Bake, uncovered, at 325°F. for about 1 hour. During last 15 minutes, heat soup and mushrooms. Spoon over baked souffle. Sprinkle with Parmesan cheese. Place under broiler 2 minutes to melt cheese. Makes 12 servings.

SHRIMP IN SHRIMP BOATS

Shrimp is always a favorite, and this double dose makes it twice as good.

1 lb. jumbo prawns, 16-20 per lb.
1/2 lb. cooked tiny bay shrimp
4 ozs. ricotta cheese
2 green onions with tops, sliced
1/2 tsp. dill
1/2 tsp Worcestershire sauce

2 tbs. Parmesan cheese, freshly grated
2 tsp. cream style horseradish sauce
1 tsp. lemon juice
salt and pepper to taste
paprika

Butterfly prawns: pull off shells but leave tails on. Carefully cut through the back of each prawn without going all the way through, removing sand vein. Flatten out as you place prawns on a broilerproof pan. Mix remaining ingredients except paprika. Top each prawn with mixture, dividing evenly. Broil for 7-10 minutes until the "boat" is firm. Sprinkle with paprika. Makes 4 servings.

SCAMPI ALLA ROMANA

Use the largest available shrimp and serve with crusty bread to soak up the marvelous garlic butter.

20-24 jumbo or super jumbo shrimp
1/2 cup butter
2 cloves garlic, minced
4 shallots, or 1/2 cup green onion, thinly sliced
1 tbs. lemon juice

1 tbs. Worcestershire sauce
dash cayenne pepper
1 tbs. fresh parsley, chopped
1/4 cup dry white wine

Peel and devein shrimp, leaving tail attached. Melt butter; add garlic and onion. Stir in lemon juice, Worcestershire sauce, cayenne pepper, parsley and wine. Place shrimp on a heat-proof platter or broiler pan. Pour 1/2 garlic butter mixture over shrimp. Broil 5″ from heat for 3 minutes. Turn shrimp over, pour remaining garlic butter mixture over and broil 3 minutes longer. Allow shrimp to marinate 2 minutes before serving. Makes 4 servings.

GLAZED SHRIMP KABOBS

1 lb. raw large shrimp
  (14 to 16 per pound)
12 lime or lemon wedges
1/4 cup apricot preserves

1/4 cup orange juice
1/4 cup lemon juice
2 tbs. honey
2 tsp. cornstarch

2 drops hot pepper sauce
1/2 tsp. dried mint
4 skewers

Thaw shrimp if frozen. Peel raw shrimp leaving tails on. Remove sand veins and wash. Thread the following on metal or bamboo skewers which have been soaked a few minutes in water: a lime or lemon wedge, 2 shrimp, a lime or lemon wedge, 2 more shrimp and another citrus wedge. Cover tails of shrimp with aluminum foil. Place kabobs on a tray, cover and refrigerate until ready to cook. To prepare glaze, combine preserves, orange and lemon juice, honey, cornstarch, and hot pepper sauce. Stir until no cornstarch lumps remain. Cook, stirring constanting until mixture thickens slightly. Simmer 3 to 4 minutes. To broil kabobs place on well-greased broiler pan. Brush with sauce and sprinkle with mint. Broil about 4 inches from source of heat for 5 minutes. Turn, brush with sauce and sprinkle with mint. Broil 4 to 5 minutes longer or until shrimp turns pink and is lightly browned. Remove foil from tails and serve with remaining sauce. Makes 2 to 3 servings.

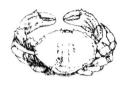

SHRIMP AND RICE

1 lb. peeled and deveined shrimp
2 tbs. lime or lemon juice
1/2 tsp. ground cumin
1 small garlic clove, mashed
1/2 tsp. salt
1 tbs. minced onion
2 tbs. butter
1 cup chicken broth

1 cup long grain rice
1 medium onion, thinly sliced
2 tbs. olive oil
1 can (16 ozs.) Italian style tomatoes
1 cup clam juice
1 small bay leaf
dash pepper
3 tbs. chopped parsley

Thaw shrimp if frozen. Mix lime juice with cumin, garlic and salt. Pour over shrimp. Cover and marinate 1 to 2 hours. In a Dutch oven cook the minced onions in butter until golden. Add chicken broth and rice. Bring to a boil, reduce heat and simmer 5 minutes. Cook sliced onions in olive oil in a large saucepan. Add tomatoes, clam juice, and seasonings. Boil together 10 minutes. Remove shrimp from marinade. Add marinade to tomato mixture. In a large frypan cook and stir shrimp, adding oil if necessary, until they turn pink. Arrange shrimp over rice in Dutch oven. Spoon tomato sauce over shrimp and rice. Sprinkle with parsley. Cover and bake in a 375°F. oven for 35 to 40 minutes or until liquid is absorbed by rice. Makes 4 servings.

SHRIMP MORNAY

You may prepare this ahead of time and simply pop it under the broiler for a few minutes when you are ready to serve it.

1 lb. raw shrimp, cooked, shelled and deveined (see page 43)
  or 1/2 lb. frozen large shrimp, defrosted;
  or 2 cans (4-1/2 ozs. each) canned shrimp, rinsed and drained
2 tbs. butter
2 tbs. flour
1/3 cup milk
1 cup chicken broth
1/4 cup shredded Swiss cheese
1/4 cup grated Parmesan cheese

Prepare shrimp. Melt butter over medium-high heat. Add flour. When bubbly, stir in milk. Add broth. Slowly stir in Swiss cheese. When thick, add shrimp. Divide into four ramekins or baking shells. Top with Parmesan cheese. Broil four inches from heat until bubbly hot and lightly browned. Makes 4 servings.

SHRIMP AND ARTICHOKE CASSEROLE

1 lb. fresh shrimp, shelled and
    deveined (see page 43) **or** 3/4 lb. frozen
    medium shrimp, defrosted
6 tbs. butter
2 tbs. cornstarch
2 cups milk
1 tsp. salt
1/4 tsp. pepper
1 tbs. Worcestershire sauce

dash Tabasco
1/4 cup dry sherry
1 can (14 ozs.) artichoke hearts
    or 1 pkg. frozen, cooked
1/2 lb. fresh mushrooms, sliced
1/4 cup grated Parmesan cheese
paprika
rice to serve 6

Prepare shrimp. Melt 4 tablespoons butter in saucepan. Blend in cornstarch. Add milk. Boil one minute. Add salt, pepper, Worcestershire sauce, Tabasco and sherry. Drain artichokes, cut in half. Arrange in shallow, greased casserole. Scatter shrimp over artichokes. Melt remaining butter, add mushrooms and saute. Add to the shrimp. Pour white sauce over all. Sprinkle with cheese and paprika. Bake at 350°F. for 20 to 30 minutes. Serve over rice. Makes 6 servings.

SHRIMPLY DELICIOUS

This dish is also known as Shrimp Harpin. You can assemble it a day ahead.

2 lbs. large, fresh shrimp, shelled
and deveined (see page 43)
1 tbs. lemon juice
3 tbs. salad oil
3/4 cup rice, cooked
2 tbs. butter
1/4 cup minced green pepper
1/4 cup finely chopped onion
1 tsp. salt

1/4 tsp. white pepper
1/4 tsp. mace
dash cayenne pepper
1 can (10-1/2 ozs.) tomato soup, undiluted
1 cup heavy cream
1/2 cup dry sherry
1/2 cup slivered almonds
paprika

Place shrimp in large greased casserole. Drizzle lemon juice and oil over shrimp. Gently toss rice with shrimp. In separate pan, melt butter. Add green pepper and onion. Saute 5 minutes. Add salt, white pepper, mace, cayenne, tomato soup, cream and sherry to sauted mixture. Gently stir into shrimp and rice. Cover mixture and refrigerate overnight. Before baking, top with almonds and sprinkle with paprika. Bake at 350°F. for about 25 minutes. Makes 8 servings.

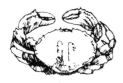

CHINESE SHRIMP AND CHICKEN

If you have any leftover chicken, try this low calorie dish.

2 tbs. butter
1-1/2 cups diagonally sliced celery
1/4 cup finely chopped onion
1 lb. fresh, raw shrimp, peeled
    and deveined (see page 43)
1 cup sliced, fresh mushrooms

2 cups diced, cooked chicken
1 tbs. cornstarch
2 tbs. soy sauce
1 cup chicken broth
2 cups bean sprouts, **or**
    2 cups fresh chopped spinach

Melt butter in skillet over medium heat. Add celery and onion. Cook 2 minutes. Add shrimp and mushrooms. Cover and cook 2 minutes. Add chicken. Remove pan from heat. Mix together cornstarch, soy sauce and broth. Return pan to heat. Add sauce and cook over medium-high heat until thickened and clear. Add sprouts. Cook 1 minute. Serve immediately. Makes 6 servings.

OYSTER LOAVES

Fried oyster sandwiches are as popular in the south as Hoagies, Poor Boys, and Submarines are in the north. In fact, some small shops sell them exclusively.

2 dozen oysters, shucked and
    well drained (see page 45)
1 cup yellow cornmeal **or**
    finely ground bread crumbs
1 tsp. salt
1/4 tsp. pepper

1/8 tsp. cayenne
salad oil
1/4 cup melted butter (optional)
4 rolls or sandwich buns
Garnishes: pickle slices, hot sauce, catsup or
    cocktail sauce (optional)

Rinse oysters and pat dry. Combine cornmeal, salt, pepper and cayenne. Roll each oyster in crumb mixture to coat evenly. Heat one inch of oil to 375°F. Fry oysters about 1 minute on each side, or until golden brown. Drain on absorbent paper. Slice rolls lengthwise. Arrange oysters on bottom half of each roll. Garnish as desired. Top with upper half. Serve immediately. Makes 4 servings.

HANGTOWN FRY

Legend has it that a goldminer who just "struck it rich," rode into town one day, strutted into the restaurant and shouted, "Gimme the most expensive thing on your menu!" An imaginative cook came up with this clever recipe utilizing two of the most rare and expensive ingredients in his mountainous, western town—eggs and oysters.

12 to 18 oysters, shucked if fresh, (see page 45), drained if bottled
salt and pepper to taste
3/4 cup finely ground cracker crumbs

7 eggs
4 tbs. butter
1/4 cup milk or cream

Sprinkle oysters with salt and pepper. Roll in cracker crumbs. Beat 1 egg well. Dip cracker covered oysters in egg. Roll in cracker crumbs again. Melt butter in large frying pan. Add oysters and brown lightly, 2 to 4 minutes. Beat remaining eggs with milk. Season with salt and pepper. Pour eggs into frying pan. Cook eggs and oysters slowly, over low heat, until eggs are set. When done, slide onto a serving platter and fold in half. Makes 4 servings.

SCALLOPED OYSTERS

A perfect dish for brunch, lunch, late dinner or a buffet. Easterners have been preparing oysters this way for generations.

1 qt. shucked oysters (see page 45) in their liquor
4 tbs. cream
1 tsp. Worcestershire sauce
1 cup soft, white bread crumbs
2 cups cracker crumbs
1 cup melted butter

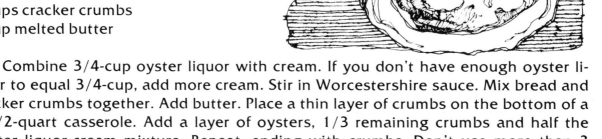

Combine 3/4-cup oyster liquor with cream. If you don't have enough oyster liquor to equal 3/4-cup, add more cream. Stir in Worcestershire sauce. Mix bread and cracker crumbs together. Add butter. Place a thin layer of crumbs on the bottom of a 1-1/2-quart casserole. Add a layer of oysters, 1/3 remaining crumbs and half the oyster liquor-cream mixture. Repeat, ending with crumbs. Don't use more than 2 layers of oysters. Bake at 400°F. for 30 minutes. Makes 6 to 8 servings.

SOUPS

There are many different names for soup, especially when you're talking about seafood soup. Fish stock is the most clear of all seafood soups. It is identical to broth, consomme and bouillon in consistency. And, like these soups, it is used as a "base" in sauces, main dishes and stew soups. Chowder is a combination of fish or shellfish, vegetables, herbs, spices and, usually, milk or cream. The most hearty and filling of all seafood soups are gumbos and seafood stews. Gumbo, which originated in the south, is distinguished by its file powder. File powder is made from the young leaves of the sassafras tree and was introduced to the French Colonists by the Choctaw Indians. When stirred into any liquid it binds and thickens. Most gumbos and seafood stews, such as bouillabaisse, consist of a mixture of fish and shellfish in a rather spicy, thin tomato based broth.

While the best meat soups are made after long hours of slow cooking, this is definitely not the case with seafood soups. Even the fish stock, on which the most hearty seafood stews are based, needs only minimal cooking. You might simmer the tomato broth for a stew for an hour or so, but don't add the seafood until the last few minutes of cooking.

Any of these soups may be served as an appetizer, first course or main dish.

CRAB AND SPINACH SOUP

This delightfully easy soup is the perfect addition to a Chinese banquet.

1/2 lb. fresh crabmeat or 1 (6 ozs.) can crab, drained, flaked, cartilage removed
6 cups chicken broth
1/2 cup onion, chopped
3 tbs. dry sherry
1 tsp. fresh gingerroot, grated
1/2 tsp. salt
1/4 tsp. white pepper
4 cups fresh spinach, washed, deveined, cut into shreds

Rinse and pick over crab. In a Dutch oven, combine chicken broth, onion, sherry, gingerroot, salt and pepper. Bring to a boil. Add spinach leaves and crab. Cover and simmer 5 minutes. Makes 8 servings.

Bouillabaisse (page 133) ▶

NEW ENGLAND CLAM CHOWDER

30 fresh chowder clams, **or** 2 cups canned clams
4 slices bacon, diced
1/2 cup diced onions
1/2 cup chopped celery
4 medium potatoes, peeled and diced
water

2 cups light cream
salt and pepper to taste
1/2 tsp. oregano
1/8 tsp. marjoram
1/4 tsp. thyme

If you are using fresh clams, shuck them (see page 31). Reserve the liquor, or juice, from each clam. If you are using canned clams, drain them and reserve their liquor also. Chop clams coarsely. Fry bacon in skillet until crisp. Remove from pan and drain on paper towels. Reduce heat in pan, add onions to bacon grease, and fry until tender. Add celery. Cook for 3 minutes more. Add potatoes, reserved liquor and enough water to cover potatoes. Simmer for 25 to 30 minutes, or until potatoes are tender. Add clams and cook for 3 minutes. Reduce heat to low and slowly add cream, bacon, salt, pepper, oregano, marjoram and thyme. Heat until just warm. Do not boil, or cream will curdle. Makes 8 servings.

◀ Crab Louie (page 142)

MANHATTAN CLAM CHOWDER

1 pint clams, **or** 2 cans, 8 ozs. each
4 strips bacon, diced
1/2 cup chopped onion
1/2 cup chopped celery
1/4 cup chopped green pepper
2 cups diced potatoes

1/4 tsp. sage
1/4 tsp. thyme
1-1/2 tsp. salt
dash cayenne
3 cups canned tomatoes,
    crushed, with juice

Drain clams, reserving liquor. Chop coarsely. Fry bacon over medium heat until it renders most of its fat. Don't let it become crispy. Add onion, celery and green pepper. Cook about 5 minutes, or until tender. Add clam liquor to measuring cup. Add enough water to equal one cup. Add potatoes and seasonings. Cook 15 to 20 minutes, until potatoes are tender. Add clams and tomatoes with juice. Heat until just warm. Makes 6 servings.

CHUNKY FISH AND POTATO SOUP

Chunks of potato and fish in a dill-flavored broth makes great soup.

5 cups chicken broth
2 lbs. mixed fish fillets **or** steaks
   (ling cod, sole and red snapper are good choices)
1 large onion, finely chopped
1 lb. red or new potatoes, cubed

1 tsp. dill weed
1 cup heavy cream
salt and pepper to taste
6 tbs. butter, cut in 6 slices
1/2 cup chopped green onions

In a large saucepan heat chicken broth to boiling. Reduce to a simmer. Add fish and cook 10 minutes per inch, measured at it's thickest point (see page 14). Set pan off the heat and allow to cool for at least 20 minutes. Then lift fish out of broth with a slotted spoon. Remove and discard any skin and bones. Cut fish in bite-size chunks. Bring broth to boil over high heat. Add onion, potatoes and dill weed. Boil, un-covered, about 10 minutes or until potatoes are tender when pierced. Add cream, fish, salt and pepper to taste. Serve steaming hot in individual bowls. Add one piece of butter to each bowl. Sprinkle with green onions. Makes 6 main dish servings.

CIOPPINO

This popular West Coast dish of crab, shrimp, clams and fish is ideal for informal entertaining. Provide each guest with a large bib. Serve with lots of crusty French bread, a tossed salad, and a fresh fruit for dessert. You may vary the fish according to what your local market offers.

1/4 cup olive oil
1 medium onion, chopped
4 stalks celery, thinly sliced
4 medium carrots, thinly sliced
6 cloves garlic, minced
1/4 cup chopped parsley
1 can (1 lb. 12 ozs.) solid pack tomatoes,
    or 4 large, fresh tomatoes, chopped
2 cans (8 ozs. each) tomato sauce
1-1/2 cups water or clam juice, or combination
1 cup dry sherry
1 lemon, thinly sliced

1-1/2 tsp. **each** sweet basil, marjoram, oregano and thyme
salt and pepper to taste
1-1/2 lb. firm, white fish, cut into bite-sized pieces (flounder, turbot, halibut)
1 lb. raw prawns or shrimp, in shell
2 lbs. clams in shell, well scrubbed
1 or 2 Dungeness, or 4 to 6 blue crabs, cooked, cleaned and cracked (see page 34)

Heat oil in large kettle or Dutch oven. Add vegetables. Saute until tender, about 10 minutes. Add remaining ingredients, except fish and shellfish. Simmer gently 1-1/2 hours. The broth will have the best flavor if it is prepared one day in advance. 20 minutes before serving, add fish and shellfish to simmering broth. Cover and cook 20 minutes. Discard any clams that have not opened. To serve, ladle some of each kind of fish into warm soup bowls. Top with broth. Make it easy on your family or guests and serve extra bowls to discard shells in. Finger bowls, in which to wash your hands, would be nice also. Makes 8 servings.

# SEAFOOD GUMBO A LA BUNDY

There are many versions of Gumbo. The traditional, southern method uses a roux (a "paste") made from oil and flour. This produces a somewhat heavy flavor, which many non-southerners are not used to. For a lighter taste, use butter instead of oil. The Commander's Palace, a fine restaurant in New Orleans, uses no roux at all. The chef there prefers a simple seafood broth. You should be able to find gumbo file at almost any gourmet foods store.

2 lbs. fresh crabmeat
1 lb. raw shrimp
1 pint shucked oysters (see page 45)
3/4 cup oil or butter
2/3 cup flour
1 cup chopped onion
4 cloves of garlic, minced
1 can (16 ozs.) tomatoes, chopped
1 bay leaf

1 tsp. chopped parsley
1-1/2 tsp. salt
1 sprig thyme (or 1/8 tsp. ground)
1 hot pepper pod, **or** dash cayenne
1-1/2 lbs. fresh okra, sliced **or**, 2 pkg. frozen sliced okra
1/4 tsp. gumbo file powder
boiled rice to serve 10

Pick out and discard any cartilage in crabmeat. Shell and devein shrimp (see page 43). Drain oysters and reserve their liquor. In a large soup kettle, bring 3 quarts of water to a boil. In a separate pan, heat oil or melt butter. Add flour. Heat until mixture bubbles. If you are using oil, mixture must turn a dark brown. Do not let it burn, however. Add onions and garlic. Cook over low heat 4 minutes. Add roux to boiling water. Add tomatoes, bay leaf, parsley, salt, thyme, pepper, okra and oyster liquor. Simmer over very low heat at least 2 hours. Gumbo may be prepared up to this point a day in advance. 20 minutes before serving, add seafood. 5 minutes before serving, add gumbo file. Serve in warm soup bowls over rice. Makes 10 servings.

LANDLUBBER'S CHOWDER

1 lb. shark steaks
3 strips bacon
1 cup chopped onion
2 cans (10-3/4 ozs. each) condensed
  cream of potato soup
2 cups milk
1 can (1 lb.) stewed tomatoes

1 pkg. (10 ozs.) frozen mixed
  vegetables, thawed
1 can (8 ozs.) whole kernel corn, drained
1 tsp. salt
1/8 tsp. pepper
1 small bay leaf

Thaw fish if frozen. Cut into chunks. Fry bacon in Dutch oven until crisp. Drain bacon on absorbent paper and crumble. Cook onion in bacon drippings until tender. Add soup, milk, tomatoes, vegetables, corn, salt, pepper and bay leaf. Heat, stirring occasionally, until simmering. Add fish and bacon. Simmer fish 10 minutes per inch of thickness (see page 14). Makes 9 cups chowder.

BOUILLABAISSE

2 lbs. fin fish (red snapper, haddock, flounder, rock **or** sea trout, **or** combination)
1/2 to 1 lb. shrimp, lobster, scallops, crabmeat, **or** combination
18 small clams, mussels, oysters, **or** lobster claws, in their shells
1/4 cup olive oil
1 large onion, finely chopped

2 shallots, minced
4 cloves garlic, minced
2 cups fish stock, clam juice, **or** chicken broth
1 can (13 ozs.) tomatoes with liquid
2 tsp. salt
dash cayenne
1/2 tsp. **each** thyme, basil and saffron
chopped parsley (optional)

Cut fish into bite-sized pieces. Shell shrimp, lobster or crab if desired. (Traditionalists prefer to leave the shells on during the cooking process. They believe it gives the stew a better flavor.) Scrub clams, mussels, oysters or lobster claws well. Heat oil. Saute onions, shallots and garlic about 10 minutes. Add liquid, tomatoes and seasonings, except parsley. Lower heat and simmer 15 minutes. Add all seafood. Cover and cook 10 minutes. Discard any clams that have not opened. Serve in large bowls, sprinkled generously with parsley. Makes 6 servings.

 # QUICK FISH STOCK

Avoid using strong-flavored fish such as mackerel, bluefish or skate.

1 fresh, medium-sized uncooked fish skeleton and head
1 tsp. salt
1/4 cup vinegar

Scrape as much flesh from skeleton as possible. Poach in 4 cups of boiling water, salt and vinegar for 1 minute. Remove bones. Cool. Reserve liquid. If there is any flesh on the skeleton, pull it off and reserve it. Return bones to liquid. Simmer for 15 minutes. Discard skeleton. Strain liquid. Return fish pieces to liquid. Refrigerate and use within three days. May be frozen in air tight containers up to 6 months. Makes about 4 cups.

COURT BOUILLON

Court bouillon is a flavored liquid in which fish can be poached.

2 qts. water
1 cup dry white wine
1/2 cup white **or** tarragon vinegar
2 stalks celery, chopped
2 carrots, chopped
1 onion stuck with 5 cloves
1 sprig dill
1 tsp. **each** tarragon, chives, thyme, chervil **or** parsley
4 whole peppercorns
1 tbs. salt

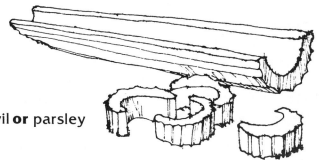

Combine all ingredients and simmer for 30 minutes. May be used immediately or strained and refrigerated for a few days. Double or triple recipe as needed. Makes 2 quarts.

SALADS

When it's hot outside and you don't feel like cooking, why not put together a seafood salad? These recipes are quick and easy to prepare. Many of them can be assembled ahead for an added time saver.

Seafood salads are a natural for dieters or people just trying to "eat light." The low-calorie protein found in seafood, coupled with the vitamins found in the other vegetables or fruits, make seafood salads a well-rounded meal.

When you are serving seafood salads, make sure all the ingredients are the freshest possible. Nothing is worse than limp lettuce. For really perfect salads, chill the salad plates and forks. Make your salads lovely to look at as well as delicious with attractive garnishes.

 # LOMI LOMI SALMON SALAD

Known as the official luau salad in Hawaii, it is perfect anytime the juicy red tomatoes are in season and you want something unusual on your menu.

1/2 lb. salted salmon
5 tomatoes, diced
10 green onions, sliced thin
1 medium onion, finely chopped
1 cup crushed ice

Soak salmon in water to cover overnight. Drain. Remove skin and bones. Using fingers, shred the flesh. (Lomi lomi means to massage, which is what you do as you shred the salmon.) Combine salmon, tomatoes and onions and gently mix together. Chill thoroughly. Add ice just before serving. Makes 6 servings.

 # TUNA AND ARTICHOKE SALAD

This hearty salad is perfect on a hot summer night, or to take on a picnic.

1 pkg. rice and vermicelli mix, chicken flavor
2 (6 ozs. each) jars marinated artichoke hearts
6 green onions with tops, sliced
1/2 green pepper, chopped
2 (6-1/2 ozs. each) cans tuna in water, drained
1/2 cup low calorie mayonnaise
1/2 cup plain yogurt or reduced calorie sour cream
1 tsp. curry powder

In a medium pan, combine rice-vermicelli mix, contents of seasoning packet and 2-1/2 cups water. Bring to a boil, cover and simmer for 15 minutes. Cool. Drain artichokes, reserving marinade from one jar. Combine artichokes, green onion, green pepper and tuna with rice. Combine marinade, mayonnaise, yogurt and curry powder. Gently fold dressing into rice mixture. Chill several hours. Makes 8 servings.

 # ARTICHOKES IN A SHRIMP RING

Leftover salad can be added to a tossed salad the next day for a new zing.

2 (3 ozs. each) pkg. lemon gelatin
2 cups boiling water
1/2 tsp. salt
2 cups V-8 vegetable juice or tomato juice
4 tbs. lemon juice
2 tbs. grated onion
3 drops hot pepper sauce

1/4 tsp. sweet basil
1/2 lb. fresh bay shrimp, cooked
2 ripe avocados
1/2 cup celery, diced
1 (6 ozs.) jar marinated artichoke
    hearts, drained
salad greens

Stir gelatin into water. Add salt and stir to dissolve. Add vegetable or tomato juice, lemon juice, onion, pepper sauce and basil. Chill until mixture congeals. Add shrimp, 1 avocado peeled and diced, and celery. Pour into a 2-quart ring mold and chill. Unmold onto salad greens. Peel and dice remaining avocado, combine with artichoke hearts and fill center of ring. May be served with a small bowl of mayonnaise lightened with whipped cream. Makes 8 servings.

 # BOUILLABAISSE SALAD

1/4 lb. cooked crab or lobster meat
1/2 lb. cooked medium-size shrimp, deveined
1/4 lb. cooked scallops (if large, cut into 1/2-inch cubes)
1/2 lb. cooked fish, cut into bite-size pieces
1 small head lettuce or mixed salad greens torn into pieces
melon balls, or other fruit
strawberries, or other fruit
Louie Dressing, page 142
wafers or crackers

Combine fish and shellfish. Arrange over salad greens in a shallow serving bowl or small platter. Garnish with melon balls, strawberries or other fruit and serve with wafers or crackers. Pass the Louie Dressing. Makes 4 servings.

CHINESE SEAFOOD SALAD

Prepare the salad and dressing the day before. Add the fried noodles just before serving. To stretch for 10 to 12 servings, add more pineapple and a larger can of noodles.

1 can (6 ozs.) crab, drained
1 can (4-1/2 ozs.) shrimp, drained
4 eggs, hard boiled and sliced
3/4 cup celery, chopped
1/4 cup chopped green pepper
1/2 cup sliced green onions with tops

1 can (8-1/4 ozs.) pineapple cubes, drained
1 cup mayonnaise
1/4 cup red wine vinegar
1 can (3 ozs.) fried Chow Mein noodles,
   or rice noodles
lettuce

Remove any cartilage from crabmeat. Mix crab, shrimp, eggs, celery, green pepper, onions and pineapple. Mix together mayonnaise and vinegar. Pour over crab mixture. Refrigerate overnight. Just before serving add noodles and toss gently. Serve on lettuce leaves. Makes 8 servings.

◀ Paella (page 104)

# CRAB OR SHRIMP LOUIE

On the West Coast, this is a favorite way to serve crab or shrimp. Sour dough French bread and white wine complete the menu.

1 large cooked Dungeness crab or
  2 cups small cooked shrimp, deveined
lettuce leaves
endive
tomato wedges
hard-cooked eggs
black olives
lemon wedges

Louie Dressing:
  1 cup mayonnaise
  2 tbs. parsley
  2 tbs. chili sauce
  1 tbs. catsup
  1 tsp. Worcestershire sauce
  1 tsp. A-1 steak sauce

Crack crab and pick out meat. Combine all ingredients for Louie Dressing. Chill until needed. Arrange lettuce and endive on chilled salad plates. Spoon crabmeat or shrimp in center of greens. Garnish with tomato wedges, hard-cooked eggs, olives and lemon wedges. Pass Louie Dressing. Makes 4 servings.

 # CITRUS SEAFOOD SALAD

Any firm white fish, local to your area, may be used in this recipe. Shrimp is also delicious prepared this way.

2 cups fresh fish fillets,
   or 2 cups cooked and cleaned shrimp
2 grapefruits, peeled, cored and sectioned
2 oranges, peeled, cored and sectioned
1/4 cup chopped green onions, with tops
salad greens
1/2 ripe avocado, peeled and sliced

Salad Dressing:
1/4 cup **each** vinegar, oil and catsup
2 tbs. sugar
1 tsp. chili powder
1 clove garlic, mashed

Poach fish in simmering, salted water for 8 to 10 minutes. Cool in liquid. When cold, remove from liquid and debone. Chill. Mix together grapefruit and orange sections. Add onion. Chill. Combine all ingredients for salad dressing. Just before serving, combine fish with fruit mixture. Moisten with salad dressing. Arrange greens on plates. Scoop salad onto greens. Garnish with avocado slices. Makes 4 servings.

SEAFOOD MOUSSE

Want to impress your guests at your next party? Pour this mousse into a fish mold. Turn it out onto a large platter lined with lettuce. A super spectacular!

1-1/2 cups crab, lobster **or** tuna,
   or any combination of these
1 cup finely chopped celery
1/2 cup finely chopped green pepper
   or cucumber
1/4 cup finely chopped green onion,
   with tops
1 tsp. salt
1/4 cup lemon juice

1 tbs. Worcestershire sauce
1 can (10-1/2 ozs.) tomato soup, undiluted
1 small pkg. (3 ozs.) cream cheese
3 envelopes unflavored gelatin
1 cup cold water
1 cup mayonnaise
lettuce, enough for large platter
tomato wedges, for garnish
cucumber slices, for garnish

Drain and flake seafood. Combine with celery, green pepper, onion, salt, lemon juice and Worcestershire sauce. In the top of a double boiler, mix together soup and cream cheese. Simmer over water until cheese melts. Soften gelatin in cold water. Add gelatin to soup mixture. Simmer over water until gelatin dissolves. Cool. Stir in mayonnaise and seafood mixture. Spoon into a 1-1/2-quart fish or ring mold. Chill several hours, until firm. Just before serving, dip mold briefly in hot water, to loosen. Invert onto platter that has been lined with lettuce. Garnish with tomatoes and cucumber slices. Makes 8 servings.

 ## HERRING POTATO SALAD

A pleasant change from ordinary potato salad.

2 cups diced, boiled potatoes
1 cup diced, pickled herring fillets
3/4 cup chopped celery, with leaves
1 tbs. minced parsley
1 tbs. minced chives

1/3 cup sour cream
1-1/2 tbs. lemon juice
1/2 tsp. paprika
lettuce leaves to serve 6

Combine all ingredients except lettuce leaves, and toss gently. Arrange lettuce leaves on chilled salad plates. Spoon salad onto lettuce. Makes 6 servings.

SAUCES

If you live in an area which has a narrow selection of seafood, don't despair. A good repertoire of sauces, like the ones contained in this chapter, will help you avoid boredom. A simple Herb Butter Sauce, which can be prepared in minutes, will perk up any baked, broiled or fried fish.

The most important thing to remember when you are planning to serve a sauce with your seafood is that the sauce should enhance, rather than cover up, the flavor of the seafood. Delicate seafoods need only subtle enhancement such as my Tartar or Cucumber Sauce will give. More flavorful seafood with darker colored meat goes well with Mustard Sauce.

 ## GINGER SOY MARINADE

This basic marinade is good for any fish you plan to grill, broil or bake.

2/3 cup soy sauce

1/3 cup dry sherry

1 clove garlic, minced

1-1/2 tsp. fresh gingerroot, grated

3 small green onions, minced

1 tsp. lemon zest (peel), grated

1 tbs. lemon juice

Mix all ingredients in a dish with a tight cover or a sealable plastic bag. Add fish and marinate for 30-60 minutes, turning frequently. Cook as directed. Makes 1-1/4 cups for up to 2 lbs. fish.

 **BASTING SAUCE**

A piquant sauce for basting your favorite pan fried, broiled or baked fish.

4 tbs. butter, melted
4 tbs. lemon juice
4 tbs. catsup

1/2 tsp. seafood seasoning
1/2 tsp. salt

Mix all ingredients. Makes 3/4 cup.

 **TARTAR SAUCE**

1/2 cup **each** mayonnaise and sour cream
1 tsp. lemon juice
few drops Tabasco

1 tbs. **each** finely chopped stuffed green olives, sweet pickle, onion, capers and parsley

Mix all ingredients and chill 30 minutes. Makes 1-1/2 cups.

 # SEAFOOD COCKTAIL SAUCE

A perfect "topper" for any fresh shellfish.

1/2 cup ketchup **or** chili sauce
1 tbs. diced onion
2 tbs. lemon juice
2 tsp. horseradish

1 tsp. Worcestershire sauce
dash Tabasco sauce, if desired
salt to taste

Combine all ingredients. Chill at least 1 hour before serving. Makes 4 servings.

 # MUSTARD SAUCE

Serve with any fried seafood.

1/2 cup mayonnaise
1 tbs. Dijon mustard

1 tbs. vinegar

Combine ingredients. Makes 1/2 cup.

HERB BUTTER SAUCE

3 tbs. tarragon vinegar
2 tsp. chopped shallots
1/4 cup butter
1 tbs. chopped chives

1 tbs. chopped chervil **or** parsley
1/4 tsp. thyme
1/8 tsp. fennel seed

Combine vinegar and shallots in a saucepan. Bring to a boil. Add remaining ingredients. Serve with cooked fish. Makes 1/2 cup.

CUCUMBER SAUCE

3 large cucumbers
2 tsp. salt
1 cup sour cream
  or unflavored yogurt

1 cup mayonnaise
1/2 tsp. dill
1 tbs. vinegar
dash garlic powder

Peel, halve and seed cucumbers. Chop very fine. Mix with salt. Chill at least two hours. Drain well. Add remaining ingredients. Chill. Makes 3-1/2 cups.

 **TROPICAL SALSA**

Break away from tartar sauce with this delightful healthy accompaniment. You will love it with chicken as well as with mild or strong fish. (Also, see **Pineapple Salsa**, page 65).

1 each papaya and mango, peeled
1/2 cup red onion, cut to 1/4″ dice
1 serrano or jalapeno chile, seeded, minced
1 tbs. salad rice vinegar
1 tsp. dried pepper flakes
1/8 tsp. salt
1/4 cup cilantro, finely chopped
1 grapefruit, sectioned
1 orange, sectioned

1 cup strawberries, hulled, diced
1/2 cup cantaloupe
    or other melon, diced
1/2 cup green pepper, diced
1 tbs. lime juice
1/4 cup fresh mint leaves,
    finely chopped
1/4 cup macadamia nuts, chopped
    (optional)

Prepare at least one hour before serving to "marry" flavors. Dice fruit over a bowl to save juices. Cut all fruit about the same size. Blend all ingredients except cilantro and nuts, if used. Add these just prior to serving. Salsas may be made up to three days ahead but should be served at room temperature. Makes enough to garnish 4-6 servings.

INDEX